Louisiana's French Heritage

Truman Stacey

Acadian House
PUBLISHING
LAFAYETTE, LOUISIANA

ABOUT THE COVER: LaSalle claims the vast Louisiana territory for France in April of 1682, as other Frenchmen, Indians and missionaries look on. (Details can be found in Chapter 20.)

— Illustration by Robert Dafford, Lafayette, Louisiana

©Copyright 1990 by Acadian House Publishing, Inc.

Published by:
ACADIAN HOUSE PUBLISHING
Lafayette, Louisiana

ISBN: 0-925417-02-5

Printed in the United States of America

Introduction

Louisiana's French Heritage is the story of the French contribution to the colonization of the New World during the period running roughly from 1500 to 1800. It describes the settlement of the Acadian Peninsula, the discovery and exploration of the Mississippi River, the development of the first Louisiana colony, and the persecution and exile of the French-Acadian people from their homeland in the mid-1700s.

It was the fishing business that first brought the French to the New World, and it was the fur trade that motivated them to permanently sink their roots into the soil of the Acadian Peninsula, known today as Nova Scotia. They were attracted to the interior of the continent by tales of rich copper and silver fields; by hopes of finding the great Father of Waters, which the Indians said flowed southward to the warm sea; and by the desire to spread the Christian faith which they themselves embraced.

As much as anything, *Louisiana's French Heritage* is an adventure story. It describes the trials and tribulations of the French pioneers in the wilderness, how they learned to live off the land with the help of the Micmac Indians, how they survived the bitter-cold winters of North America, their skirmishes with hostile Indians, and their fruitful dealings with friendly tribes. The story deals with the French pioneers' fears and their fearlessness, with their frustrations in trying to carve civilization out of the wilderness, and with their eventual and resounding triumphs.

The narrative provides an insight into the age-old theme of man's inhumanity to man: It deals with the religious and political persecution of the Acadians by the British, and with the callous slaughter of Indian men, women and children by the sadistic Iroquois.

Conversely, it provides glowing examples of the goodness and decency of which human beings are capable, such as the Spanish government's benevolence in helping the exiled Acadians in Europe find homes for themselves in Louisiana after being homeless for 30 years.

The author details LaSalle's successful quest to reach the Gulf of Mexico by way of the Mississippi River. And he delves into the adventures of other Frenchmen who explored parts of the continent before LaSalle – such as Champlain, Marquette and Joliet – and many who came after him – such as Iberville, who picked up where LaSalle left off; Saint Denis, the founder of Natchitoches; and the Robidoux brothers, who explored nearly the entire West.

Louisiana's French Heritage also explains the early, discouraging efforts to colonize Louisiana and the obstacles that the colonial leaders had to overcome: hurricanes and floods, hostile Indians and inadequate supplies from the mother country, not to mention an uncomfortable percentage of colonists who were about as equipped to be colonists as babes are to live in the woods.

And, finally, the author documents the contributions made by the French in opening up the American West. In doing so, he provides a clear insight into the tireless nature of the true explorer and his unquenchable thirst to see what is over the next hill.

–TRENT ANGERS,
Editor

Foreword

This book is a revised and expanded edition of the magazine version of *Louisiana's French Heritage*. The work first appeared as a 35-part newspaper series in the *Lake Charles (Louisiana) American Press* in 1972. It was published as a single, lengthy article in *Acadiana Profile* Magazine in 1975, then reprinted in the magazine in 1981 and 1987 due to popular demand.

The text in most chapters is essentially the same as it originally appeared, except for minor revisions. The major changes occur in chapters 32 and 33, which deal with the Acadian exile and with the contributions of Frenchmen who explored the American West. These are expanded versions of material in the author's original work.

Other new material includes the cover painting by Robert Dafford of Lafayette, La., all the illustrations appearing in the book, the bibliography, and the separate story on the late Jimmie Domengeaux, founder of the Council for the Development of French in Louisiana (CODOFIL), the man to whose memory this book is dedicated. (The author wrote the book in 1972 after becoming fascinated with the history of the French in Louisiana while he was working with CODOFIL, the state agency dedicated to the preservation of Louisiana's French language, heritage and culture.)

Chapter 32, titled "The Acadians' Trans-Atlantic Migration of 1785," is an expanded account of the exile and resettlement of some 1,600 displaced Acadians following years of wandering and rejection in Europe. This chapter contains, among other things, the names and occupations of the Acadian heads of households who made the voyage from France to New Orleans.

Chapter 33, "Trailblazers of the Western Lands," is a more extensive account of the adventures and achievements of French trappers, traders and explorers who were forerunners of civilization in the American West. These men founded towns, forts and trading posts; they made contact with formerly unknown groups of Native Americans; they extended the fur trade westward to the Rocky Mountains and beyond.

–T.A.

In memory of
JAMES (JIMMIE) DOMENGEAUX,
who displayed an extraordinary degree
of pride in his French-Acadian heritage
and who was the founder
of the Council for the Development of French
in Louisiana (CODOFIL).

(A story on Mr. Domengeaux's life
and achievements can be found starting on page 170.)

Acknowledgements

The editor acknowledges with appreciation: Melinda Flynn, Billy Gunn and Linnie Herpin, for their patient assistance in the research phase; Tom Sommers, the commercial artist who worked long and hard to prepare the book for the printer; Randy Haynie, who granted us permission to use a painting from his collection on the cover; and John Magill of The Historic New Orleans Collection, who helped us locate several of the illustrations used in the book.

Table of Contents

PART I: Pioneers in the New World

1. The day of the mariner 13
2. Frenchmen learn the ways of the Micmac people 18
3. Adventures in New World living......................................21
4. Trading with the natives 25
5. The beginnings of New France 28
6. Growing pains in the New World 34
7. The first families of Acadia..38
8. The census of 1671 41
9. An era of prosperity in Acadia, 1671-1710 48

PART II: Exploring the Continent

10. Settling on the St. Lawrence 55
11. Warlike Iroquois trade furs for guns 58
12. The advent of the *coureurs de bois* 61
13. Europeans pulled into Indian tribal warfare 63
14. Converting the red man to Christianity 67
15. Iroquois make and break the peace – again 74
16. Adventures in westward expansion 77

PART III: LaSalle and the Father of Waters

17. The great explorer begins his quest 83
18. LaSalle and Tonti push on despite sufferings and hardships 88
19. The Great Expedition 92
20. LaSalle claims Louisiana for France 96

PART IV: The Colonization of Louisiana

21. Iberville takes over from LaSalle..................................101
22. 'Re-discovering' the Mississippi 104
23. First French colony in Louisiana set up at Biloxi Bay 107
24. Getting familiar with the Mississippi Valley 110
25. Louisiana territory taken over by proprietor......................114
26. The birth of New Orleans 117

27. Germans greatly aid colonization effort 120
28. Life goes on in the new colony as Bienville
   is made governor again..123

PART V: The Acadian Exile & Resettlement in Louisiana

29. Acadians forcibly deported from their homeland..................129
30. Exiles treated badly in British colonies 132
31. Displaced Acadians finally settled in Louisiana 136
32. The Acadians' trans-Atlantic migration of 1785 139

PART VI: Epilogue

33. Trailblazers of the Western lands....................................157

About the author 169
James Domengeaux: Congressman, lawyer and leader
   of a cultural revolution 170
Bibliography...183
Index 185

Louisiana's French Heritage

Part I

Pioneers in the New World

Samuel de Champlain founded Quebec, the first permanent
settlement in New France. So great was his contribution to the
colonization of the French territory in North America that he is often
referred to as "The Father of New France."

✤

CHAPTER 1

The day
of the mariner

It all began late in the Fifteenth Century, when the men of Europe were becoming better acquainted with the sea, at a time when sailing ships were being improved and navigational aids were being developed.

The Italians, who had for centuries dominated the sea lanes of the Mediterranean, led the way in developing better marine and navigational techniques. Italian mariners became widely sought after by all of the courts of Western Europe.

One such mariner, from Genoa, sailing under the banner of Ferdinand and Isabella of Spain, reported that he had reached the shores of India by sailing west into the Atlantic Ocean. He brought back native tribesmen and exotic plants to prove his claim.

Other mariners began to cast reflective eyes toward the west. They reasoned: If one sailor could get to India by sailing west, why not others? Other sovereigns, apprehensive that Spain might come to control all of the trade with the Orient, began to lay their own plans for trading expeditions. Merchants of the Atlantic coastal nations began to awaken to the possibilities of profitable relations with those strange climes to the west.

Among these were merchants of Bristol, on the west coast of England.

They decided to finance an exploration and trading expedition, and they had just such a man as they needed in their employ. He was Giovanni Caboto, a Genoan like Columbus, who had spent many years in Venice as a trading captain. With the blessings of King Henry Vll, Caboto (The British called him John Cabot, since that was easier to spell and to pronounce.) set sail from Bristol in May of 1497, in the ship "Mathew," manned by a crew of 18.

Rounding Ireland, Caboto headed north and then west. After 52 days at sea, he made landfall at what is now Cape Breton Island. Caboto was convinced he had found the northeast shore of Asia, but it was a forbidding coast, and no rich Asians were to be found. Small vessels of the day did not linger long on unknown coasts, and the "Mathew" soon sailed back to Bristol, arriving home in August.

Caboto was disappointed that he had not discovered the Great Khan and rich cities, and so were his merchant backers. King Henry Vll somewhat grudgingly presented him with 10 pounds sterling (That would be about $50 today.) for "having found the new isle."

Caboto and his men made one discovery, however, that was to have far-reaching effects upon the future history of Europe. They discovered the Grand Banks of Newfoundland and its enormous supply of codfish.

When Caboto's seamen reached home and dispersed after the voyage, it was natural for them to spread tales about the shoals which teemed with fish.

It was not long before fishing vessels from France were tempted to test the fishing in New World waters. Records show that the first Norman fishing vessel showed up at the Grand Banks in 1504, and it was not long after that mariners from Dieppe, Rouen, Le Havre, Fécamp, Harfleur and Honfleur were making annual voyages to the Grand Banks.

French mariners soon were making two trips annually to New World waters. They set out in late January or early February, braving the North Atlantic winter, and returned as soon as their holds were full. Then, in April or May, they were off again, returning to France again in September.

In the early years, fish were taken, cleaned and put in the hold between thick layers of salt. This was "wet" fishing. It was not long, however,

❝ Caboto and his men made one discovery that was to have far-reaching effects upon the future history of Europe. They discovered the Grand Banks of Newfoundland and its enormous supply of codfish. ❞

> *The first Norman fishing vessel showed up at the Grand Banks in 1504.*

before mariners discovered that the cod could be sun-dried on land. Cured cod was tastier than the salt variety and easier to handle.

Curing the codfish necessitated establishing depots ashore, however, and the French began to go ashore each summer at some snug harbor or inlet on an island or along the coast. The French, the Portuguese and the English established depots on Newfoundland, on the Acadian Peninsula at Canseau and La Heve, on Cape Breton Island, and at Tadousac, on the St. Lawrence River.

Once the ships arrived at the chosen depot, they would be unrigged for the season. The crew went ashore to cut timber and build platforms, or stages, which extended out into the sea.

The actual fishing was done in small boats manned by four or five men. When they returned with boatloads of fish, they threw their catches upon the stages. There they were cleaned, salted and dried in preparation for the trip back to France.

Eastern half
of North America
in the 1700s

Anticosti Island

Newfoundland

Gulf of St. Lawrence

St. Lawrence River

Prince Edward Island

Cape Breton Isla

Lake Superior

Quebec

St. John River

Wisconsin River

Green Bay

Montreal

Bay of Fundy

LaHeve

Acadian Peninsula

Grand Pré

Lake Michigan

Lake Huron

Ottawa

Port Royal

Cape Sable

Mississippi River

Illinois River

Lake Ontario

Lake Erie

Boston

New York

Missouri River

Ohio River

Philadelphia

Arkansas River

Mississippi River

Red River

Charleston

Savannah

Baton Rouge

Mobile

Biloxi

Pensacola

New Orleans

Gulf of Mexico

W e s t

I n d i e s

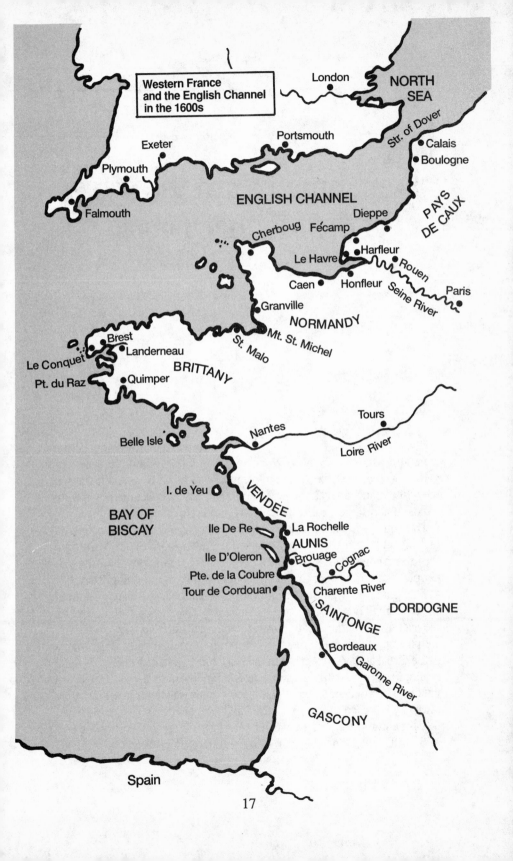

Western France
and the English Channel
in the 1600s

London
NORTH SEA
Str. of Dover
Calais
Boulogne
Portsmouth
Exeter
Plymouth
ENGLISH CHANNEL
PAYS DE CAUX
Falmouth
Dieppe
Cherboug
Fécamp
Harfleur
Le Havre
Rouen
Caen
Honfleur
Seine River
Paris
Granville
NORMANDY
Brest
St. Malo
Mt. St. Michel
Le Conquet
Landerneau
BRITTANY
Pt. du Raz
Quimper
Tours
Nantes
Loire River
Belle Isle
I. de Yeu
VENDÉE
BAY OF
BISCAY
Ile De Re
La Rochelle
AUNIS
Ile D'Oleron
Brouage
Cognac
Pte. de la Coubre
Charente River
Tour de Cordouan
DORDOGNE
SAINTONGE
Bordeaux
Garonne River
GASCONY
Spain

17

CHAPTER 2

Frenchmen learn the ways of the Micmac people

When the French fishermen first began to venture ashore in the New World to dry their fish, or hunt for game, or gather fresh berries, they came in contact with the natives. At the time of the white man's arrival, the Acadian Peninsula was occupied by roving bands of aborigines, called Micmacs by today's scholars.

The Micmacs were of the Algonkin language family and enjoyed a hunting and food-gathering culture of the more primitive sort. At the time the French began to live in the New World, there were about 3,000 of these people, wandering over the Acadian Peninsula and adjoining islands.

They had only rudimentary social organizations, and they wandered about in small bands, which were in actuality only large families. Mostly they set their wanderings to coincide with their food supply.

In the spring, they left their camps along the inland lakes and streams in the forest and wandered about the seashores, gathering clams, oysters, scallops and other seafood at low tide. Some of the more adventurous even ventured into deeper waters to hunt seals, walrus and porpoise, and they always welcomed the return of the vast numbers of codfish.

In the autumn, they returned to the forests, tracking down spawning eels in the tidal rivers, and later in winter turning their attention to moose hunting and beaver trapping. Caribou, otter and bear were also coveted game.

The bow and arrow formed the Micmacs' chief hunting weapon, and they also used a wide variety of traps and snares. Their dogs played an important role in the hunt.

Vegetable food was generally plentiful, but the Micmacs seem to have utilized vegetables only during times of meat shortage.

The birchbark canoe was perhaps the most efficient transportation vehicle developed in North America, and all of the Eastern tribes used it. The craft was relatively easy to construct, was very light in weight and shallow in draft, yet an ordinary canoe was capacious enough to hold a household of five or six persons, their dogs, sacks, skins, kettles and other baggage. The canoe was particularly suited for inland routes where water was shallow and portages from a few yards to a mile or more were common.

In winter, the Micmacs traveled on snowshoes, which excited French curiosity from the beginning. They likened them to the tennis rackets they used in France.

With these tools, the Micmacs were able to wander where they pleased, and they astounded the French with their knowledge of the topographical features of the country. When they moved through country they had previously traversed, their memory for the lay of the land was uncannily accurate. They also passed knowledge from one to another by means of crude bark maps.

The conical wigwam, familiar to all schoolchildren, was the generally used shelter by the Micmacs. Its array of supporting poles was used to support overlapping strips of bark. Sometimes, mats woven of swamp grasses were used instead of bark. Animal skins were used as entrance flaps, and for the more affluent, or for the more successful hunters, might be used to cover the entire wigwam.

Household equipment such as cups, dippers and boxes were made of birch bark, until trade with the French brought iron utensils to the Micmacs. The Micmacs used furs and skins for their clothing, and there were almost no differences in the dress of the sexes.

The Micmacs were not warlike, and they set up a friendly relationship

---

❢ *In winter, the Micmacs traveled on snowshoes, which excited French curiosity from the beginning. They likened them to the tennis rackets they used in France.*❢

---

with the French. Since the early settlers confined themselves almost exclusively to the tidal marshes and did not invade the forest, there were few occasions for clashes.

The Micmacs were useful to the French chiefly as guides, canoemen, hunters and fur trappers. Their ties with the French were reinforced by a slow but ultimately almost universal attachment to the Roman Catholic religion.

They were also useful in providing valuable lore on fishing and hunting, the knowledge of local nuts, roots, berries and grasses, the making of clothing and footwear from skins, the making of fibers from roots and animal sinews, and the use of dyes from a wide variety of vegetable sources.

Had there been no Micmacs on the Acadian Peninsula at the time of the French settlement, that settlement would probably have come much later, and it would have been much more difficult, and its historical significance may well have been altered drastically.

CHAPTER 3

Adventures in New World living

French fishermen who sailed to the Grand Banks for their shiploads of cod and other fish also brought back home accounts of the forests, rivers and beaches of the new lands westward. And the courts of Europe buzzed with the tales of the vast treasures the Spaniards were finding in Mexico.

Other crowned heads began to consider the New World awaiting exploitation. They were intrigued by the tales of the gold the Spaniards had won. They mused over the trading advantages that would accrue to the nation that discovered the fabled Northwest Passage to India.

King Francis I of France was one of these rulers who decided that France should not be left out of this pursuit of riches and glory. Most of the kings of Europe at that time employed Italian artists, scientists and navigators to add a luster of culture to their courts. King Francis was no exception.

He selected a Florentine shipmaster, Giovanni da Verrazano, to spearhead the ventures of France in the New World. Verrazano sailed from Madeira in 1524 aboard "La Dauphine," a small ship with a crew of 50 Normans.

Verrazano was driven off his course and arrived at the coast of the

New World, probably near the mouth of the Cape Fear River. He sailed northward along the coast, exploring the littoral as far as Cape Race before returning to Dieppe.

His return was celebrated at court, but Francis found himself too entangled in European problems to do much about Verrazano's discoveries.

A decade passed before another French official took up the task of New World discovery. In 1534, Jacques Cartier sailed from St. Malo as an agent of the Admiral of France, Philippe de Brion-Chabot, on a voyage of reconnaissance.

Cartier rounded Newfoundland and passed through the Straits of Belle Isle, erected a wooden cross at Gaspé and ascended the mouth of the St. Lawrence River as far as an Indian village called Anacosti. Convinced that he had discovered the Northwest Passage, he returned to France.

His reports opened such glowing possibilities that Admiral Chabot commissioned Cartier to undertake a second voyage. King Francis invested 3,000 livres in the enterprise. This time Cartier departed in the spring of 1535 with three ships and 110 men.

By Aug. 13, this expedition had sailed beyond the westernmost point of his first voyage, and, leaving the bulk of his expedition at Anacosti, Cartier and 30 men ascended the St. Lawrence River to the Indian village of Hochelaga, at the foot of a mountain that Cartier named Mount Royal, and which is the current site of Montreal.

The Indians told Cartier that there was another great river to the west, and a land where the natives wore European clothing, lived in towns and possessed great stores of copper and silver.

The next day they returned to their base, and there built a small fort on the site of present-day Quebec. This fort is about two degrees south of the latitude of Paris, and Cartier and his men had no way of knowing that winters in the New World would be different than winters in France.

The shock they received from the mid-November snows must have been overwhelming. The river froze solid, imprisoning the ships. Snow-drifts sometimes climbed mast-high. Ice four inches thick covered the ship decks and riggings. Sub-zero winds howled without surcease across the frozen river.

As if that were not enough, scurvy struck. By mid-November only a dozen of the 110 men were still healthy, and 25 died before the Indians showed the French a remedy made by the bark and needles of white cedar boiled in water. This tonic revived the ill.

When the winter of misery ended, Cartier and his men returned to France. After the king received his report, the crown selected Jean François de la Roque, Sieur de Roberval, to head the next expedition,

The Indians told Cartier that there was another great river to the west, and a land where the natives wore European clothing, lived in towns and possessed great stores of copper and silver.

which the king hoped would be able to plant a colony in the New World. Cartier was to be his chief captain. In order to get the necessary manpower for his squadron, Roberval was empowered to ransack France's prisons and to conscript anyone he wished.

The expedition was not prepared in time, however, and Cartier sailed in 1541, expecting Roberval to follow. Once more Cartier reached the mouth of the St. Lawrence, and there began to prepare for the coming colonists. Roberval did not weigh anchor until April of 1542, however, and when his ship sailed into the harbor of what is now St. John, Newfoundland, he found Cartier there, the latter having abandoned the attempted colonization and preparing to sail for France.

Roberval ordered Cartier to return to the St. Lawrence, but the captain slipped anchor in the night and sailed for France. Roberval continued to the St. Lawrence and there constructed a barrack for his colony at the Indian village of Tadousac, where visiting fishermen and fur traders had built a few shacks.

Experience in New World living was absent, however, and so was wisdom. Nothing went right for the new colony. In 1543, the king sent Cartier out once again, this time to rescue Roberval and his survivors.

The Marquis de la Roche was the next proposed colonizer, and he too was given permission to make a French lodgement in the New World. In 1588, he landed a group of colonists, mostly convicts, on Sable Island, off present-day Nova Scotia.

Contrary winds drove La Roche's ship out to sea, and he returned to France. It was not until 1603 that another vessel was dispatched to look for the survivors of the Sable Island colony. The rescuers found 11 gaunt, bearded men, whom they returned to France.

In 1600, a merchant of St. Malo named François Grave, Sieur de Pont (sometimes called Pontgrave), went into partnership with Pierre Chauvin, a sea captain, in the hopes of doing some profitable trading in the New World. Chauvin took a small vessel up the St. Lawrence to Tadousac. Chauvin landed 16 men to winter here, while he sought a shipload of furs. He returned to France in the fall.

When he returned to Tadousac the following spring, he discovered that the 16 men he had left had found it impossible to subsist in the grim win-

Cartier and his men had no way of knowing that winters in the New World would be different than winters in France. The shock they received from the mid-November snows must have been overwhelming. The river froze solid, imprisoning the ships. Snowdrifts sometimes climbed mast-high. Ice four inches thick covered the ship decks and riggings. Sub-zero winds howled without surcease across the frozen river.

ter months. Most of them had died and the few survivors had joined the Indians.

By now, a new king had assumed the French throne— Henry IV—and it fell to him to supervise the actual establishment of New France. He had a number of reasons for doing so, one of the most important being the growing profitability of the fur trade with the Indians.

✤

CHAPTER 4

Trading
with the natives

As the fishing boats from France became regular visitors to the Grand Banks, they began to congregate at rendezvous points along the coast, where they dried their fish ashore during the winter months.

Some of these rendezvous points were St. John's, in Newfoundland; Tadousac, near the mouth of the St. Lawrence River; Canseau, at the tip of the Acadian Peninsula; and La Heve, farther down the peninsula.

During their stay ashore during the summer months, some of the French struck up a brisk but informal trade with the Indians. The native tribes soon developed a taste for the white man's artifacts, and were avid for iron knives, axes and pots, as well as cloth and all manner of trinkets.

Each summer, the number of Indians who came to the coast to trade increased. French seamen began to realize that they could turn a nice profit on this trade and, in fact, might clear more profit with considerably less labor than went into the unpleasant chores of drying or salting fish.

Soon ships were sailing from France bent on the fur trade alone. As a staple, furs were superior to fish in a number of ways. They were light in weight, and their value in relation to bulk was high. They were easy to package, easy to transport, and there was no danger of spoilage, as with fish.

Best of all, there was little labor involved. The Indians trapped the animals, skinned carcasses, cured the furs and brought them to the coast.

The growing popularity of the broad-brimmed felt hat in Europe was a boon to the fur trade. The fur of the beaver was the best material for making felt. By the Sixteenth Century, however, the beaver had become all but extinct in Western Europe, and only limited supplies came in from Russia and Scandinavia.

Beaver flourished in North America, and the cold Canadian winters made the animals grow a thicker, more luxurious fur than those with which Europeans were familiar.

The Indians used beaver pelts to make robes to wear and to sleep in. The sweat and grease of their bodies and the smoke of their lodges made the furs soft and supple, and thus easy to process in making felt.

In the early days of the fur trade, a knife, an axe or a few trinkets worth a couple of dollars in France could be traded for a robe that would bring more than $200 in Paris.

With such huge profits available, the fur trade grew apace, and the Indians soon learned not to trade with the first ship that arrived, but to wait until several had appeared to compete with each other.

This kind of competition quickly reduced the profits, and the fur traders began to seek rules and regulations to govern the trade. Also, French officials began to look with covetous interest upon the trade.

The crown quickly decided that if there were so much profit to be made, then some enterprising merchant would be willing to pay the crown a handsome sum for a monopoly of the trade.

That was the situation when the new king, Henri IV, began to take an interest in the New World. One of Henri's early supporters had been Aymar de Chastes, Commander of the Order of St. John. The king gave de Chastes a patent to settle a French colony in the New World.

De Chastes chose a young French soldier, Samuel de Champlain, fresh from adventures in New Spain, to make a survey.

De Chastes had formed a corporation made up of the principal merchants of Rouen to finance his New World venture. One of these was Pontgrave, who had been associated with Chauvin's earlier venture at Tadousac.

Pontgrave was to command the ship that was to take Champlain to the New World to make his survey. The little expedition sailed on March 15, 1603, and on May 6 made first landfall at Newfoundland. On May 24, the vessel arrived at Tadousac.

After concluding peaceful overtures with the Indians and promising them friendship and aid, Pontgrave and Champlain sailed up the river to Sault St. Louis, stopping en route at Hare Island (so named by Cartier) and

> *French seamen began to realize that they could turn a nice profit on the fur trade and, in fact, might clear more profit with considerably less labor than went into the unpleasant chores of drying or salting fish.*

a narrow neck of the river the Indians called Quebec.

During his voyage, he questioned the neighboring Indian tribesmen whom he met and gathered information about lakes Ontario and Erie, the Detroit River, Niagara Falls and the rapids farther up the St. Lawrence.

After a return to Tadousac, the expedition sailed along the southern lip of the St. Lawrence before returning to France. Havre de Grace was reached on Aug. 16, 1603, after a passage of 35 days.

Pontgrave and Champlain were saddened to learn upon their return that the old soldier, Aymar de Chastes, had died a few weeks earlier. The death of de Chastes would almost certainly have meant the end of the French colonization effort had not Champlain become so interested in the project that he determined to promote it with the king. He was successful in keeping Henri's interest alive.

Henri decided upon Pierre de Gua (also called de Guast), Sieur de Monts and governor of Pons, as the man to take up the task de Chastes surrendered in death. De Monts had served under Henri in the religious wars, and was a Huguenot. He was commissioned "lieutenant general of New France," was given a monopoly of the fur trade for ten years and was obliged to settle a colony of 60 people in New France.

De Monts was not a stranger to the New World. He had visited Tadousac with Chauvin in 1600, and that experience had caused him to determine that a successful colony could only be settled farther south, away from the dread northern winters.

It was to fall to de Monts and Champlain, therefore, to form the actual beginnings of New France, which in time was to include Louisiana and a dozen other states of the American union.

CHAPTER 5

The beginnings of New France

Pierre de Gua, the Sieur de Monts, was a hard-headed businessman. He was determined that his venture into New France would be properly backed. He formed a stock company among the merchants of Rouen, St. Malo, La Rochelle and St. Jean de Luz.

He fitted out two ships, which sailed from Le Havre in March of 1604. On board were de Monts himself, Pontgrave and Champlain. There was also Jean de Biencourt, Sieur de Poutrincourt, a nobleman of Picardy and a substantial investor, who had decided to accompany the first voyage west.

Having been rebuffed by the Canadian winters, de Monts determined to set up his quarters farther south, where the climate was known to be less severe. He chose La Cadie, or Acadia, a vague region then said to extend from Montreal south to the area of what is now Pennsylvania. The word is probably a corruption of a Micmac Indian word, "quoddy" or "caddy," meaning a place or a piece of land.

It was a long voyage, made uncomfortable by the fact that most of the 100 "colonists" were recruited in the usual way, from prisons and from among the vagabonds of the road.

The two ships finally reached the entrance of the Bay of Fundy and explored it. They must have been awed by the 60-foot tides that rage in those restricted waters. They sailed into Annapolis Basin, and all hands were struck by its harbor facilities and the green-lined shores.

De Monts decided, however, to plant his headquarters on an island (now Dotchet Island) across the Bay of Fundy at the mouth of a river he called the St. Croix, so that he might erect a fort there to command the entrance of the bay.

It was an unfortunate choice, because few of those on hand were really prepared for a Canadian winter untempered by the warming strands of the Gulf Stream. Once more the settlers suffered from the cold. The houses were small shelter against the cold. Cider and wine froze in the casks and had to be served by the pound. Nearly half of the colonists died of scurvy during that first winter.

Warned by this experience, de Monts took advantage of the spring to move the colony back across the Bay of Fundy to the Annapolis Basin, where he established a post named Port Royal. De Monts had granted this area to Poutrincourt, but the latter and Pontgrave had gone back to France for more settlers and supplies.

During the summer, Pontgrave arrived from France with more supplies and with 40 additional men. In the fall, de Monts himself returned to France with a number of workers whose contracts had expired and with the furs that the party had gathered. Pontgrave and Champlain remained through the winter, during which scurvy took another 12 men.

In July of 1606 Poutrincourt arrived at Port Royal aboard the "Jonas" with more men, more supplies and some livestock. The little colony fared well enough in the winter, although another seven men met death through scurvy.

The colonists by now had some home-grown wheat and vegetables to supplement the supplies from France, and judging from Champlain's journal, not all was hardship. In fact, Champlain organized a society of gourmets from among the leaders, called "the Ordre de Bon Temps."

In the spring of 1607, however, disaster struck. Word came from de Monts in France that his fur monopoly had been rescinded, and Poutrincourt was directed to abandon the Acadia enterprise and return all hands to France. On Aug. 11 of that year, the glum colonists boarded ship to return to France. Some of them may have elected to remain on their own, to live with the Micmacs and hunt and fish and trap furs, but if so their names are not recorded.

Poutrincourt, once in France, set about finding new financial backers and applied in his own right for trading rights in Acadia.

It took Poutrincourt two years to gain financial backing of a group of merchants of Dieppe. He returned early in 1610 with his two sons, Charles de Biencourt and Jacques de Salazar. He was also accompanied by a business associate, Claude de la Tour de Saint-Etienne, and the latter's 17-year-old son, Charles, as well as a chaplain, Rev. Jesse Fleche, and 23 other men.

Within a few months, Father Fleche had baptized a Micmac chief, whom the French called Memberton, and 21 of his followers.

Later in the year, Poutrincourt sent his son, Charles de Biencourt, back to France for more food supplies for a colony which had not yet learned a great deal about living off the land in the New World.

The French authorities decided to send out two Jesuit missionaries to aid in conversion of the Indians, but the Protestant merchants of Dieppe who had financed Poutrincourt's venture objected, refused to advance any more credit and called in their loans to Poutrincourt.

Young Biencourt, caught in this religious-financial tangle, turned for assistance to Antoinette de Pons, Marquess of Guercheville, who had an influential position as lady-in-waiting to the French queen, Catherine de Medici.

The marquess agreed to pay off the Dieppe merchants and to obtain funds for more supplies. In return, she asked that two Jesuits, Rev. Ennemond Masse and Rev. Pierre Baird, be allowed to sail back to Acadia to establish Indian missions.

On Jan. 16, 1611, Biencourt and his party set sail aboard the "Grâce à Dieu," bound for Acadia. He was accompanied by 36 men and his mother, Madame de Poutrincourt, who thus became one of the first European women to visit the New World.

The voyage was a difficult one, and for four months the weary party was buffeted by storms, adverse winds and icebergs, before they finally dropped anchor at Port Royal.

When the Marquess de Guercheville agreed to provide finances for the Poutrincourt colony in Acadia, she was motivated to do so because she was interested in the spiritual welfare of the Indians.

Before long, however, disputes broke out between Poutrincourt and his son, Biencourt, and the Jesuit missionaries sent to the colony by the marquess. Poutrincourt was a Huguenot and a businessman, interested in gathering furs. The Jesuits, of course, were Catholics chiefly concerned with establishing an Indian mission.

When she heard of this dispute the Marquess de Guercheville decided to withdraw her support of the Poutrincourt colony and establish one of her own. Poutrincourt went back to France to work out better terms, but could not dissuade the marquess.

In 1613, therefore, she sent out "Le Fleur de May," with 50 persons on board, to settle a colony called Saint-Sauveur, located near the present-

> *Having been rebuffed by the Canadian winters, deMonts determined to set up his quarters farther south, where the climate was known to be less severe. He chose La Cadie, or Acadia, a vague region then said to extend from Montreal south to the area of what is now Pennsylvania. The word is probably a corruption of a Micmac Indian word,"quoddy" or "caddy," meaning a place or a piece of land.*

day Penobscot, in Maine.

By now, the English, who had finally managed to establish a colony in Virginia in 1607, learned of the French colonies to the north. They deemed these colonies intrusions upon territory gained by the voyage of Caboto.

Thomas Dale, the governor of Virginia, authorized an English free-booter, Samuel Argall, to destroy the French colonies. Argall, with a small fleet, in 1613 attacked the colony at Penobscot, killed one of the Jesuits there, burned all of the buildings, took some prisoners back as slaves to Virginia and set 16 others adrift at sea in a small boat. The latter were rescued by a fishing vessel in an unusual stroke of good luck.

Argall then turned to Port Royal and did the same thing. Fortunately, most of the settlers were inland on a fur-trading mission, while the others were several miles up the Annapolis Valley, tending fields. Argall burned the colony's buildings and took off with the livestock and all the provisions that could be found.

Meanwhile, Poutrincourt was able to secure more financial backing from merchants in La Rochelle and finally arrived back in Port Royal on March 21, 1614. He immediately departed for France, carrying the colony's cache of furs. Going back to France with him was Louis Hebert, an apothecary who had spent four years in Acadia.

While attempting to work out the colony's salvation, Poutrincourt became involved in a civil war that ripped France apart. Both he and his son, Jacques de Salazar, were killed in a battle against the Prince de Conde.

Hebert sought out that other Acadian veteran, Samuel de Champlain, and asked his help to found a colony on the St. Lawrence River. This was later to become Quebec.

The death of Poutrincourt left his son, Charles de Biencourt, in charge of Port Royal, and Biencourt decided to stay in the New World and concentrate upon the fur trade. Biencourt and his men traded with the Indians and established observation posts along the coast.

When they had gathered enough furs, they signaled a French fishing vessel to come in to trade for ammunition and other supplies. Biencourt's force at this time consisted of his second in command, young Charles de Latour, and 20 other men.

They lived with the Indians, absorbed many of their customs, and became the first of the *coureurs de bois*. (The *coureur de bois* was a rugged, backwoodsman type who possessed a notable affinity for the wilderness and who traded with the Indians and sometimes lived with them.) Some of them married Indian wives, and their descendants today still live in Canada's eastern Indian reserves.

As a settlement, therefore, Port Royal practically ceased to exist.

Biencourt died prematurely at the age of 31 and was buried at La Prée Ronde, near Port Royal. Latour took over the enterprise, claiming that this was part of Biencourt's last will and testament.

While the French were seeking furs, the English decided to found their own colony in the north. Taking advantage of the civil war in France, King James I of England gave Sir William Alexander, a Scottish earl, a grant of all the lands north of the Massachusetts colony that had been discovered by Caboto.

In 1629, Alexander sent 100 Scottish colonists to settle on the Acadian Peninsula. They landed about five miles from the former Port Royal and built Charles Fort. The Scottish settlers remained there until 1632, when the Treaty of Saint-Germain-en-Laye sorted out the French and English possessions in the New World, and returned Acadia and Canada to France. Most of the Scottish settlers were returned to England, but a few families remained and became French subjects.

After the settlers at Charles Fort had departed, Charles de Latour, who had remained in the interior with his *coureurs de bois,* decided to renew contacts with France. When his father, Claude, came on a visit, Charles asked him to take a letter to the French court, asking that his trading rights be recognized.

Claude was captured by the English on his return voyage and was taken

---

❢ *The* coureur de bois *was a rugged, backwoodsman type who possessed a notable affinity for the wilderness and who traded with the Indians and sometimes lived with them.*❢

---

to Alexander, who offered him and his son titles of nobility in England in return for the outposts they occupied in Acadia. Claude decided to accept the English offer, but Charles indignantly refused.

Charles' trading rights, which he supposedly had inherited from Biencourt, had not been recognized in France, however, and after the Treaty of St. Germain-en-Laye, Cardinal Richelieu decided to organize a company to exploit the fur trade.

Richelieu sent his cousin, Isaac de Razilly of Touraine, to head the colony with the impressive title of "Lieutenant-General of all New France and Governor of Acadia." Razilly departed from France in 1632, with three ships and some 300 colonists.

Razilly landed his force at La Heve, on the eastern shore of the Acadian Peninsula, and then sailed around to take possession of Charles Fort and the remains of the settlement at Penobscot.

Charles de Latour resented the new governor, and Razilly, knowing of the former's influence with the Indians, wished to placate him. Razilly agreed to maintain his colony at La Heve, and leave to Latour his chief fur depot at Cape Sable.

Razilly also granted Latour fishing and hunting rights along the Saint John River in New Brunswick, where Latour built a fort he called Jemseg.

Two of Razilly's chief associates in the Acadian venture were Charles de Menou de Charnisay, Sieur d'Aulnay, and Nicholas Denys. D'Aulnay was put in charge of settlers and agricultural pursuits. Denys was charged with building up the fisheries and the fur and timber trade with France.

Thus, it finally seemed that the French in Acadia were about to embark on a period of growth and prosperity.

CHAPTER 6

Growing pains in the New World

The prosperity promised to the French venturers in Acadia under the leadership of Isaac de Razilly was short-lived. For nearly four years the new colony at La Heve prospered, then Razilly died suddenly in 1635. The death of this nephew of Richelieu, who enjoyed the confidence of the highest of French officials at home, marked the beginning of a long period of dispute in Acadia.

The trading company which Richelieu had organized to handle Acadian affairs decided that Charles de Menou de Charnisay, Sieur d'Aulnay, one of Razilly's lieutenants, was to take Razilly's place as head of the Acadian venture. This decision, of course, disappointed Charles Latour and Nicholas Denys, each of whom felt he should have been named to head the trading venture.

About a year after Razilly's death, d'Aulnay decided to move his settlement from La Heve to Port Royal, where there was more arable land.

Meanwhile, Latour's fur trade was prospering, and he was mending his political fences back in France. In 1638, Latour's backers persuaded the government to name d'Aulnay and Latour joint governors in Acadia.

Such an arrangement, between two strong and opinionated men, was destined for failure from the start. It was not long before open hostilities broke out between the two governors. Latour expropriated one of d'Aulnay's ships and, in 1640, tried a surprise attack on Port Royal with two ships.

D'Aulnay was not surprised, however, and the attack was repulsed. When d'Aulnay reported these depredations to Paris, the court revoked Latour's commission and his trading rights. D'Aulnay was named governor and lieutenant-general, and was ordered to seize Latour and return him to France for trial.

Latour barricaded himself in his fort at Jemseg and defied d'Aulnay. In 1643, Latour went so far as to contract an alliance with the hated English and, with four ships and two armed frigates, he and his allies attacked Port Royal once more. Three men were killed, seven wounded and a quantity of livestock, a shipload of furs and all supplies of food and powder were taken away.

D'Aulnay decided to go to France and plead with the court for help. In a final judgment in March 1644, the French court branded Latour an outlaw. D'Aulnay then returned to Acadia with reinforcements and orders to drive Latour out. In 1645, he launched an attack against Latour's stronghold at Jemseg. Latour was absent, visiting his English allies in Boston, but the defense of the fort was carried on by Madame Latour.

After a three-day battle, d'Aulnay's forces captured the fort. Many of Latour's men were hanged as traitors. Madame Latour herself survived the fall of the fort by only three months.

Latour, learning of the fall of the fort while in Boston, fled north to Canada, where he began a career as a pirate.

In 1647, the French crown transferred all of Latour's rights to d'Aulnay, and peace descended upon the little colony once more.

D'Aulnay was not destined to enjoy his triumphs for long, however. One of his chief projects was the building of dykes to keep sea water out of tidal marshes so as to convert them to arable farmlands. While visiting one of these operations upriver from Port Royal, d'Aulnay's canoe was swamped in a mud flat. Unable to escape from the mud, the governor died of exposure.

The death of d'Aulnay left his widow in financial straits and the colony in confusion. Back home in France d'Aulnay's creditors immediately began to call in their debts.

It was at this critical moment that the indefatigable Latour surfaced again. Sensing a prime opportunity at the death of his old enemy, Latour took a ship for France, to seek forgiveness of the crown. He used all of his old influence and his old friends and was so persuasive that King Louis XIV exonerated him for his acts of piracy and his rebellions against prior court orders. The king even made Latour governor of Acadia, as d'Aulnay's successor.

Armed with his new powers, Latour chose a merchant of Cherbourg, Philippe Mius d'Entremont, as his lieutenant, and sailed for Acadia.

On arrival, he presented his credentials to d'Aulnay's widow and demanded the return of his fort at Jemseg and all of the territory over which he had traded for furs.

The poor widow, powerless to resist, could only do as he asked. She was now left with only Port Royal and its immediate vicinity, and her creditors were powerful.

Charles d'Aulnay
Governor of Acadia

Once more Latour did the unexpected. The old rogue suddenly proposed marriage to the widow of his rival and married her on Feb. 24, 1653. He was 60 at the time. The former Madame d'Aulnay bore him several children.

His new marriage left Latour master of all Acadia except the fiefs held by Denys.

Troubles were only beginning for the colony, however. Emmanuel LeBorgne, d'Aulnay's old creditor, obtained a judgment against the d'Aulnay estate, and in 1653 sailed to Acadia to take demand judgment. LeBorgne, apparently an irascible fellow, seized two of Denys' posts, burned the settlement at La Heve and took possession of Port Royal while Latour and his new wife were at the fort at Jemseg on the other side of the Bay of Fundy.

While the Latours were planning to oust LeBorgne, war broke out between France and England, and an English fleet out of Boston sailed north to clear all the French out of Acadia. The English took Jemseg from Latour and Port Royal from LeBorgne.

Faced with this new disaster, Latour went to London to plead his cause with the new rulers of Acadia. There he succeeded in getting from the English permission to engage in the Acadian fur trade, in partnership with an heir of Sir William Alexander, the Scotsman who had previously tried to settle at Port Royal.

In 1656, Latour returned to Acadia, where he supervised his affairs until he died in 1666, at the age of 73. That left only Nicholas Denys among the leaders who had come out from France with Razilly. He was driven out of several of his posts by LeBorgne and went to France to seek judgment against his persecutor. Nothing came of this, and Denys finally died a poor man in 1688, age 90.

Conditions in Acadia went from bad to worse until 1667, when the Treaty of Breda ended the war between France and England, and by its terms Acadia was restored to France.

CHAPTER 7

The first families
of Acadia

While the vendetta between d'Aulnay and Latour for the control of the fur trade convulsed the infant colony of Acadia, and while the colony suffered during wars between French and English, those same years also saw the beginning of really permanent settlement in the colony.

Before the d'Aulnay period, the French who came to Acadia, save for the wife of a high official or two, were men only. They were contract workers, for the most part, who came out to work at the flaking sheds, or at the fur trade, or at tilling the company's fields to provide food for other laborers.

When their stint of labor had been completed, most of them returned to France, unless they were like the men of Latour, who became accustomed to the restless and dangerous life of the fur trade and ranged the forests with the Indians, becoming more savage than civilized.

By 1630, there were trading posts established—in addition to Port Royal—at Pentagouet, also in the Cape Sable area, and on the St. John River, and at Cape Breton. Scores of fishermen visited the Atlantic coves of Acadia every year, with wintering-over on the increase.

Any permanent settlement in a new land, however, needs the stability of family life, and d'Aulnay was one of the first to recognize this.

Under d'Aulnay's supervision, the first families were recruited to settle in Acadia. The governor spent a large part of his time as Razilly's lieutenant, and during his own term as governor in recruiting colonists from the seigneuries owned by him and his mother in the region of Loudunais.

The colonists landed by Razilly at La Heve in 1632 evidently contained few women. When the colonists were moved to Port Royal from La Heve in 1635, they numbered only 30 or 40, indicating that most had returned to France after completing construction of the company's headquarters and other buildings.

Shortly thereafter, probably around 1636, the first families are recorded as being brought to Acadia. A number of them arrived that year, landing at Port Royal from the ship "Saint-Jehan."

Three of these "first families of Acadia" were those of Pierre Martin and Guillaume Trahan, both of Bourgueil, and Isaac Pesselin of Champagne. There were also the Bugaret and Blanchard families from La Rochelle.

Louis Motin, one of Razilly's officials, brought his wife and his daughter, Jeanne. The latter soon became Madame d'Aulnay.

Between 1636 and the death of d'Aulnay, a number of other families were settled in Acadia. Many familiar names are included in this group, who were among the first Europeans to find true homes in the New World.

Because of the irregular education of many of those who made up the sailing lists and took the censuses, there are variations in spelling of these early family names. It was an era that gave no particular virtue to consistency in spelling, and sometimes the same family name might be rendered in two or even three different versions.

Among those families who arrived in Acadia during the early d'Aulnay period are the following:

Babin, Belliveau (Belliveaux), Bour (Bourg, Bourque), Breault (Breaux, Brot, Braud), Brun (LeBrun), Dugast (Dugas), Dupuis (Dupuy), Gaudet, Giroir (Girouard), Landry, LeBlanc, Morin, Poirier, Raumbaut, Savoie (Savoy), Thibodeau (Thibodeaux).

According to Genevieve Massignon, who has attempted to trace the Acadians to their place of origin in France, all of these families were recruited from La Chausée, near the village of d'Aulnay.

Others from the same region, according to Miss Massignon's research, were the Blanchard, Guerin and Terriot (Theriault, Theriot) families.

Arriving in Acadia during the latter part of d'Aulnay's administration were the following families:

Bergeron, Caouette (Caillouette, Cayouette), Clemenceau, Comeau (Comeaux), Corporon, d'Aigle (Daigle, Daigre), Doucet, Carceau, Gautreau (Gauthreaux), Godin (Gaudin), Gousman, Guilbault (Guilbeau),

> *Among the first families of Acadia: Babin, Bourg, Breaux, Dugas, Girouard, Landry, LeBlanc, Thibodeaux, Blanchard, Theriot, Bergeron, Comeaux, Daigle, Doucet, Gautreau, Hebert, Lanneau, Lejeune, Pellerin, Richard, Robichaux, Simon, Sire (Cyr), Vincent.*

Hebert, Henry, Lannoue (Lanneau, Lanoux), Lejeune, Pellerin, Pichet, Picot, Poirier, Richard, Rimbault, Robichaud (Robichaux), Simon, Sire (Cyr), Thebault (Thibault) and Vincent.

Charles Latour also brought a few settlers to his outposts in Acadia, principally to the fort at Jemseg. The first Bernard was André Bernard, a stonemason from Beauvoir-sur-Mer, who arrived in 1641. The family of Mius d'Entremont, Latour's lieutenant, arrived in another Latour expedition.

Some of the most popular Acadian names are not French in origin. According to some authorities, when Sir William Alexander's group of Scottish settlers were repatriated to England, a few of them remained to live among the French.

Among them were families named Peters and Paisley, which eventually became Pitre and Pellesey (Pelleset).

Roger Casey, an Irishman in French service, was captured by the English, wound up in Acadia and started the Kuessy family tree. Michael Forest arrived in Acadia during the English occupation after 1654, and remained to become progenitor of the Acadian family named Foret.

Jacques Bourgeois, d'Aulnay's surgeon, is mentioned as arriving in 1640. One Michel Boudrot (Boudreau, Boudreaux), who came to Acadia in 1642 as lieutenant general and judge at Port Royal, was the originator of a large and widespread Acadian clan.

A number of fishermen brought over by Denys to work at his posts along the Atlantic Coast also settled down to become Acadian patriarchs. One of these was Robert Cormier, who settled in the Annapolis River basin after working out his contracts with Denys.

The English occupation of 1654, of course, discouraged further immigration from France, and many of the French already in Acadia returned to the homeland.

Most of them remained, however, both because they were attached to their homes and also because Colbert, French prime minister, foresaw the return of the colony to France when peace was achieved. He ordered the settlers to remain, therefore, rather than return to France, or to go to Canada.

CHAPTER 8

The census
of 1671

The Treaty of Breda, signed in 1667, returned Acadia to the control of France, but it was not until 1670 that the French sent out a governor to take control of the colony. By this time, Colbert had assumed power in France as King Louis XIV's chief minister, and he saw a real potential in Acadia .

He set up Acadia as a crown colony, therefore, and removed it from the control of the fur traders. He named Hubert d'Andigny, Chevalier de Grandfontaine, as governor of the new crown colony.

Grandfontaine was already living in Canada and had been a companion of Tracy in that officer's expeditions to the West Indies and at Quebec. By the terms of his appointment, however, Grandfontaine was placed under the guidance of the governor of Canada, who was designated his immediate superior.

On Aug. 6, 1670, Grandfontaine set up a camp at what is now Penobscot, Maine, and sent his lieutenant, Joybert de Soulanges, to take possession of the fort at Jemseg. Grandfontaine moved on to Port Royal on Sept. 2, being accompanied by several officers of the Carignan regiment of the French Army, then stationed in Canada.

One of Grandfontaine's first acts as governor was to take a census of the colony, and the census of 1671 has become the most famous record of the "first families of Acadia." It has been widely reprinted in various accounts of Acadian history.

In 1671, Port Royal, Cape Sable and La Heve were inhabited by several familes of Acadian settlers. There were fishing outposts at Miramichi, Nipisiquit and Chedabouctou, under the control of the Denys family. The family of Mius d'Entremont occupied Pobomcoup and Pentagoet. The forts at Jemseg and Passamaquoddy were manned by garrisons.

The census of 1671 revealed that there were 61 heads of families in Acadia, as well as four widows with children. There were also a number of roving trappers and fisher folk, plus *coureurs de bois* who lived with the Indians, and colonial officials in various stations whose presence was not reflected in the official census.

Unfortunately for future historians and genealogists, the census-taker did not include the settlers at Cape Sable (estimated at 25 persons), Les Côtes de I'Est (estimated at 16), as well as those living at La Heve, Pentagoet and the fort at Jemseg.

From the census and other records it is possible to reconstruct a picture of the colony of Acadia during this period, which marked the beginning of prosperity for the Acadian pioneers.

At the time of the census the population had grown to nearly 400 persons. The settlers at Port Royal had 425 cattle, about the same number of sheep, pigs and horses, and the habitants were cultivating 400 arpents of land, not counting the natural grazing meadows.

The population at Port Royal, therefore, had already sunk deep roots in the land. Some of the heads of families were the third generation to live in Acadia. They had gained valuable experience in farming the country.

The substitution of a royal governor for the colonial proprietors who had been interested chiefly in fishing and furs meant that the needs of the colonists themselves would be given a higher priority back home in France.

Indeed, Jean-Baptiste Colbert, Louis XIV's new minister, had placed the development of New France high on his list of needed accomplishments, and he sought to give the colonists as much aid as possible from the mother country, as well as sending out additional colonists to

---

❢ *Authorities have concluded that three-fourths of all the Acadians living today, either in Louisiana or Canada, or Nova Scotia or Europe are descended from the families listed in the census of 1671.* ❢

---

strengthen Acadia against the repeated incursions of the English.

Still, the original families continued to dominate the colony. The Acadians had developed into an American type—long-lived, frugal and adapted to the land. They had large families, and they sent their sons out to clear new land for themselves.

Authorities have concluded that three-fourths of all the Acadians living today, either in Louisiana or Canada, or Nova Scotia or Europe are descended from the families listed in the census of 1671.

The census of old Acadia taken in 1671 is the earliest known record of the "First Families of Acadia." Genealogists and historians say the majority of the half-million Acadian descendants living in Louisiana today can trace their heritage to one or more of the families listed here who were living in old Acadie 85 years before the infamous dispersion and exile.

THE CENSUS OF 1671

PORT ROYAL

Jacob Bourgeois, druggist, 50; wife, Jeanne Trahan; children: Jeanne 27, Charles 25, Germain 21, Marie 19, Guillaume 16, Marguerite 13, Francois 12, Anne 10, Marie 7, Jeanne; cattle 33, sheep 24.

Jean Gaudet, 96; wife, Nicole Colleson; child, Jean 28; cattle 6, sheep 3.

Denis Gaudet, 46; wife, Martine Gauthier; children: Anne 25, Marie 21, Pierre 20, Pierre 17, Marie 14; cattle 9, sheep 13.

Roger Kuessy, 25; wife, Marie Poirier; child: Marie 2; cattle 3, sheep 2.

Michel de Foret, 33; wife, Marie Hebert; children: Michel 4, Pierre 2, Rene 1; cattle 12, sheep 2.

Widow Etiene Hebert, 38; children: Marie 20, Marguerite 19, Emmanuel 18, Etienne 17, Jean 13, Francoise 10, Catherine 9, Martin 6, Michel 5, Antoine 1; cattle 4, sheep 5.

Antoine Babin, 45; wife, Marie Mercie; children: Marie 9, Charles 7, Vincent 5, Jeanne 3, Marguerite 1; cattle 6, sheep 8.

Olivier Daigre, 28; wife, Marie Gaudet; children: Jean 4, Jacques 2, Bernard 1; cattle 6, sheep 6.

Antoine Hebert, cooper, 50; wife, Genevieve Lafrance; children: Jean 22, Catherine 15; cattle 18, sheep 7.

Jean Blanchard, 60; wife, Radegonde Lambert; children: Martin 24, Madeline 28, Anne 26, Guillaume 21, Bernard 18, Marie 15; cattle 12, sheep 9.

Widow Francois Aucoin, 26; children: Anne 12, Marie 9, Jerome 7, Huguetta 5, Francois 2; cattle 6, sheep 3.

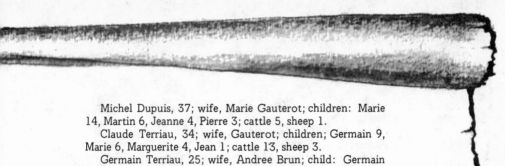

Michel Dupuis, 37; wife, Marie Gauterot; children: Marie 14, Martin 6, Jeanne 4, Pierre 3; cattle 5, sheep 1.

Claude Terriau, 34; wife, Gauterot; children; Germain 9, Marie 6, Marguerite 4, Jean 1; cattle 13, sheep 3.

Germain Terriau, 25; wife, Andree Brun; child: Germain 2, cattle 5, sheep 2.

Jean Terriau, 70; wife, Perrine Breau; children: Claude 34, Jean 32, Bonaventure 30, Germain 25, Jeanne 27, Catherine 21, Pierre 16; cattle 6, sheep 1.

Francois Savoye, 50; wife, Catherine LeJeune; children: Francoise 18, Germain 16, Marie 14, Jeanne 13, Catherine 9, Francoise 8, Barabe 6, Andree 4, Marie 2; cattle 4.

Jehan Corporon, 25; wife, Francoise Savoie; child: one daughter of 6 weeks; cattle 1, sheep 1.

Pierre Martin, 70; wife, Catherine Vigneau; children: Pierre 45, Marie 35, Marguerite 32, Andre 30, Mathier 35; cattle 7, sheep 8.

Francois Pelerin, 35; wife, Andre Martin; children: Hugette 5, Marie 3, Ann 10 months; cattle 3, sheep 4.

Pierre Morin, 37; children: Pierre 9, Louis 7, Antoine 5, Marie 3, Ann 10 months; cattle 3, sheep 4.

Mathieu Martin, 35; not married, weaver; cattle 4, sheep 3.

Vincent Brun, 60; wife, Renee Brode; children: Madeline 25, Andree 24, Francois 18, Bastien 15, Marie 12; cattle 10, sheep 4.

Francois Gauterot, 58; wife, Edmee Lejeune; children: Marie 35, Charles 34, Marie 24, Reme 19, Marguerite 16, Jean 23, Francois 19, Claude 12, Charles 10, Jeanne 7, Germain 3; cattle 16, sheep 6.

Guillaume Trahan, 60; wife, Madelaine Brun; children: Guilaume 4, Jehan-Charles 3, Alexandre; cattle 8, sheep 10.

Pierre Sire, gunsmith, 27; wife, Marie Bourgeois, child: Jean 3 months; cattle 11, sheep 6.

Pierre Thibeaudeau, 40; wife, Jeanne Terriau; children: Pierre 1 and 5 daughters; cattle 12, sheep 11.

Claude Petit Pas, 45; wife, Catherine Bagard; children: Bernard 12, Claude 8, Jean 7, Jacques 5 and 3 daughters; cattle 26, sheep 11.

Bernard Bourg, 24; wife, Francoise Brun; child: 1 daughter; cattle 6, sheep 9.

Michel Boudrot, 71; wife, Michelle Aucoin, children; Francois 29, Charles 22, Jean 16, Abraham 14, Olivier 10, Claude 8, Francois 5, 4 daughters; cattle 5, sheep 12.

Pierre Guillebaut, 32; wife, Catherine Teriau; child: 1 daughter; cattle 6, sheep 5.

Jean Labatte, 33; wife, Renee Gautherot; cattle 26, sheep 15.

Martin Blanchard, 24; wife, Francoise LeBlanc; cattle 5, sheep 2.

Jean Boure, 26; wife, Marguerite Martin; children: 2 daughters; cattle 3, sheep 5.

Antoine Boure, 62; wife, Antoinette Landry; children: Francois 27, Jean 24, Bernard 22, Martin 21, Abraham 9, and 6 daughters; cattle 12, sheep 8.

Laurent Granger, 34; wife, Marie Landry; children: Pierre 9 months and 1 daughter; cattle 5, sheep 6.

Perinne Landry, widow of Jacques Joffrian, 60.

Pierre Doucet, bricklayer, 50; wife, Henriette Peltret; children: Toussaint 8, Jean 6, Pierre 4, and 2 daughters; cattle 7, sheep 6.

Francois Boure, 28; wife, Marguerite Boudrot; children: Michel 5 and 1 daughter; cattle 15, sheep.

Germain Doucet, 30; wife, Marie Landry; children: Charles 6, Bernard 4, Laurent 3; cattle 11, sheep 7.

Francois Girouard, 50; wife, Jeanne Aucoin; children: Jacob 23, Germain 14, and 3 daughters; cattle 16, sheep 12.

Jacques Belou, cooper, 30; wife, Marie Girouard; child: 1 daughter; cattle 7, sheep 1.

Jacob Girouard, 23; wife, Marguerite Gauterot; child; Alexandre: cattle 7, sheep 3.

Pierre Vincent, 40; wife, Anne Gaudet; children: Thomas 6, Michel 3, Pierre 2, and 1 daughter; cattle 18, sheep 9.

Pierre Martin, 40; wife, Anne Ouestnorouest; children: Pierre 10, Rene 8, Andre 5, Jacques 2; cattle 11, sheep 9.

Vincent Brot, 40; wife, Marie Bourg; children: Antoine 5, Pierre 1, 2 daughters; cattle 9, sheep 7.

Daniel LeBlanc, 45; wife, Francoise Gaudet; children: Jacques 20, Etienne 15, Rene 14, Andre 12, Antoine 9, Pierre 7, and 1 daughter; cattle 17, sheep 26.

Michel Poirier, 20; cattle 2.

Barbe Baiols, widow of Saviniue de Courpon; 8 children in France and 2 daughters married in this country; cattle 1, sheep 5.

Antoine Gougeon, 45; wife, Jeanne Chebrat; child: one daughter; cattle 20, sheep 17.

Pierre Commeaux, cooper, 75; wife, Rose Bayols; children: Etienne 21, Pierre 18, Jean 14, Pierre 13, Antoine 10, Jean 6 and 3 daughters; cattle 16, sheep 22.

Jean Pitre, edge tool maker, 35; wife, Marie Mayols (first wife, Marie Peselet); children: Claude 9 months and 2 daughters; cattle 1.

Etienne Commeaux, 21; wife, Marie Lefebre; child: 1 daughter; cattle 7, sheep 7.

Charles Bourgeois, 25; wife, Anne Dugast; child: 1 daughter; cattle 12, sheep 7.

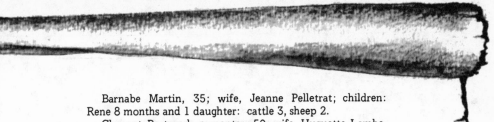

Barnabe Martin, 35; wife, Jeanne Pelletrat; children: Rene 8 months and 1 daughter: cattle 3, sheep 2.

Clement Bertrand, carpenter, 50; wife, Huguette Lambelot; cattle 10, sheep 6.

Antoine Belliveau, 50; wife, Andree Guion; children: Jean 19 and 1 daughter; cattle 11, sheep 8.

Rene Landry, 53; wife, Perrine Boure; children: Pierre 13, Claude 8 and 5 daughters; cattle 10, sheep 6.

Thomas Cormier, carpenter, 35; wife, Madeline Girouard; child: 1 daughter; cattle 7, sheep 7.

Rene Rimbaut, 55; wife, Anne-Marie; children: Phillipe 16, Francois 15, and 3 daughters: cattle 12, sheep 9.

Abraham Dugast, gunsmith, 55; wife, Marie Judith Doucet; children: Claude 19, Martin 15, Abraham 10 and 5 daughters: cattle 19, sheep 3.

Michel Richard, 41; wife, Madeleine Blanchard; children: Rene 14, Pierre 10, Martin 6, Alexandre 3, and 3 daughters; cattle 15, sheep 14.

Charles Melancon, 28; wife, Marie Dugast; children: four daughters; cattle 40, sheep 6.

Pierre Melancon, tailor, refused to answer. (He had a wife and 7 children.)

Etienne Robichaud told his wife that he did not want to give account of his cattle and his land.

Pierre Lanaux or Lanoue, cooper, sent word that he was feeling fine and he did not want to give his age.

THE HABITATION OF POBONCOM
NEAR THE ISLAND OF TOUQUET

Phillippe Mius, squire, sieur de Landremont, 62; wife, Madeleine Elie; children: Abraham 13, Phillippe 11, another of 17 and two daughters; cattle 26, sheep 25.

AT CAP NEIGRE

Armond Lalloue, sieur de Derivedu 58; wife, Elizabeth Nicolas; children: Jacques 24, Armond 14, Arnault 12 and two daughters.

AT RIVIERE AUX ROCHELOIS

Guillaume Poulet, his wife and one child.

CHAPTER 9

An era of prosperity in Acadia, 1671-1710

The colonists of French Acadia enjoyed the most prosperous era in their history during the 30-odd years between 1671 and 1710, despite repeated raids of English freebooters, who continued to descend upon the colony from time to time, burning, looting and murdering.

It was a time of growth and expansion. There was a significant infusion of new blood from France in the form of artisans, soldiers and colonists. In addition, from time to time marriageable girls came to Acadia, seeking husbands and a place for themselves in New France.

New settlements began to spring up throughout the peninsula. In 1672, Jacques Bourgeois, one of the more prosperous inhabitants of Port Royal, began to develop a settlement on one of the extensions of the Bay of Fundy known today as Cumberland Basin. The Indians called the area Chignectou.

Bourgeois had arrived in Acadia as a surgeon in 1640 under d'Aulnay's regime. He traded with the Indians in the Cumberland Basin region, where he decided to lay out farms for his two sons and three sons-in-law. Thomas Cormier, one of Bourgeois' sons-in-law, became the most well-to-do member of the new settlement.

In 1676, Michel LeNeuf de la Vallière, a Canadian from Trois Rivières, was given a grant of all the land in the Cumberland Basin, except those farms of the Bourgeois family already laid out. Vallière called the area Beaubasin.

In 1680, the first farms were cleared in the Grand Pré region in the Bassin des Minas area by Pierre Melancon of Port Royal. Two years later he was joined by Pierre Terriot, and other settlers began to flock in.

In 1689, Mathieu Martin of Port Royal, often called "the first French-man born in Acadia," was granted a parcel of land near present-day Truro. In the same year, other Acadians received land grants in the area north of Port Royal in the vicinity of the Petitcoudiac and Memramcock rivers.

Meanwhile, new settlers were arriving, both from France and from Canada. Soldiers from the Carignan Regiment, which had been shipped to Canada to fight the Iroquois, began to settle in Acadia after their terms of service. They bore such names as Leger, Lort and LaMontagne.

In the spring of 1671, the ship "L'Oranger" from LaRochelle brought out about 50 colonists recruited by Colbert. These names were noted among the newcomers: Amirault, Arcenault (Arceneaux), Barriault (Barilleaux, Barrois), Benoit, Brossard (Broussard), Doiron, Giraut (Girault, Girard) and Levron.

Colbert continued his efforts to recruit new blood for the colony, seeking to strengthen it as a barrier against the English. Between 1671 and 1686, several new family names appear in Acadian history, their owners having arrived either from Canada or France. Among them: Chaisson (Giasson), d'Amours, Dubreuil, Gourdeau, Hache (Ache), Henry, Labauve, Lapierre, Lambert, Leprince (Prince), Mercier, Mignault, Mirande, Pelletier, Pinet, Porlier and Rivet.

During the decade following 1686, names of new arrivals appearing in Acadia included: Bonneive, Blondin, Boucher, Boutin, Boisseau, Brasseau, Cellier, Champagne, Darois (DaRoy), Heon, Herpin, Lalande, Langlois, Lavergne, Mouton, Naquin, Nuirat, Olivier, Oudy (Audy), Poitevin (Potvin), Poitier (Poithier), Savary, Suret (Surrette), Tillard, Toussaint and Vignault (Venoit, Vegneaux, Vignaud).

During the last years of French control of the colony, still more newcomers were arriving in Acadia seeking lands for farms and opportunities to make their fortunes.

Among the last arrivals in French Acadia were: Allard, Allain, Barnabe, Beaumont, Babineau (Babineaux), Bideau, Cadet, Crosse, Clemenceau, Chauvert, Carre de Vaux, Dubois, Denis, Donat, Dumont, Darbone, Emmanuel, l'Esperance, Guerin, Jasmin, LaBasque, LaBreton, Lounais, Lafont, LaMarquis, LaMaistre, Lessoil, Laliberte, Laurier, Lanquepee.

Also, Moipe (Moise), Maurice, Maillard, Marceau, Maissonat, Parisien, Raymond, Roy, Rosette, Saint-Scene, Samson, Simon, de Saulnier,

Thibeau, Veco, Voyer, Villatte, Yvon.

In 1714, a census taken at Grand Pré revealed the following new names in Acadia: Aubin, Bellefontaine, Blou, Bastarche, Cochu, Desorcis, Fardel, Godin, Gareau, Levron, Laroche, LaBarre, Lalloue, Lavellee, Lagosse, Michel, Martel, Poulet, Prejean and Tourangeau.

As the population of Acadia expanded through the arrival of colonists and the growth to maturity of the children of the older settlers, more farmland was needed and more settlements were founded. Two colonies sprang up on the Petitcoudiac River in 1698. Chipoudy was founded by Pierre Thibodeau, who had come to Acadia with Emmanuel LaBorgne. Guillaume Blanchard also founded a settlement there which he named for the river upon which it was based.

Alexandre Brossard and his brother, Joseph, settled on Boundary Creek around 1740. Joseph was later to become a legendary figure in Louisiana.

By 1710, it was estimated that the population of Acadia from the St. John River to Cape Breton had increased to some 2,500 persons, a handsome increase from the 400-odd counted in the famous census of 1671.

By 1755, when the expulsion of the Acadians was begun by the English, it was estimated that the population numbered between 7,000 and 8,000.

By the beginning of the Eighteenth Century, the Acadians had adapted themselves to the New World and had learned to make full use of the country's gifts. They became adept at farming, livestock breeding, hunting, lumbering and fishing.

During the long winters they spun cloth, using either wool or flax, tanned their own leather and made their own soap and candles and fashioned their own furniture and wooden tools.

In the spring, they made maple syrup and spruce beer, of which they grew quite fond.

They were still, however, dependent upon foreign sources for metal, guns and ammunition, salt, some wearing apparel and the trinkets they used for trade with the Indians.

❝ *It was a time of growth and expansion. There was a significant infusion of new blood from France in the form of artisans, soldiers and colonists. In addition, from time to time marriageable girls came to Acadia, seeking husbands and a place for themselves in New France.* ❞

Hunting and fishing, the building of boats and small vessels, and the fur trade occupied some Acadian families, but for the vast majority the major occupation was farming.

Early in their stay in the New World, the Acadians learned to build dykes across sections of salt marshes, then drain and cultivate the land for farming.

The major crops were wheat, barley, rye, cabbage and a large variety of garden vegetables. Apples and cherries were also plentiful.

Livestock of all kinds were kept, but cattle were the most numerous. Horses were few, indicating an infrequent use of plows and poor roads. Most of the land was hand-cultivated, and the Acadians traveled by water whenever possible.

During the winter months, of course, the time was occupied by household carpentry, spinning, weaving, tanning, cobbling, the salting and smoking of meat, and the endless household chores that were the lot of women in a frontier economy.

As the population increased, so did Acadian trade with Canada, the French West Indies and France. Timber, furs, fish and flour were exported in return for manufactured goods, metals, implements, guns and ammunition that the Acadians needed. There was also an illegal, and therefore clandestine, trade with New England for some of these necessities.

Thus, after three or four generations, the Acadians had succeeded in carving out for themselves a comfortable, if not luxurious, life in the New World. They tilled their dyked fields and built their cabins on the slopes between the sea and the forests. Parents worked with their sons and sons-in-law, and daughters banded together and worked as teams.

Married sons of the same family often lived in their father's house, or nearby, and respected the father's authority. The Acadians' deference to and respect for their elders, according to contemporary accounts, seem without modern parallel.

They built churches, schools and homes and grew to love the soil upon which they toiled.

They were hospitable and cheerful and were happiest when gathered together to celebrate the rituals and the melodies of the great liturgical occasions.

Their chief weakness, it was said, was a love of gossip and a certain amount of personal vanity. Yet, according to Subercase, the last French governor of Acadia, "The more I consider these people, the more I believe they are the happiest people in the world."

Now, with the Acadians prospering in Acadia, it is time to retrace our steps, and to follow the fortunes of other French pioneers who planted the *fleur de lis* on the rocky shores of Canada.

51

Part II

Exploring
the
Continent

A French missionary and two coureurs de bois carry their canoe around a waterfall. Portaging in this fashion was routine when traveling through the wilderness of North America during the era of French exploration.

CHAPTER 10

Settling
on the
St. Lawrence

While some groups of French merchants were attempting to settle in Acadia, others were attempting to exploit the fur trade of the northern wilds by forging settlements and trading posts on the St. Lawrence River.

After his experiences in Acadia, Champlain once more turned his attention to the St. Lawrence. Champlain returned to France from his explorations in Acadia in 1607, and immediately sought out the Sieur de Monts with a proposal that further explorations be carried out in the North.

At first, de Monts was not interested, but later he was able to obtain from the crown a monopoly of the fur trade on the St. Lawrence River for a year, and in April of 1608, he dispatched an expedition of two ships to the St. Lawrence to explore and to open up the fur trade.

The two ships, "Don de Dieu," captained by Henri Couillard, and "Levrier," captained by Nicholas Marion, set sail on April 5 for Tadousac, an Indian village and trading post on the St. Lawrence. At one time, the Portuguese had set up a whaling station there.

Champlain and another Acadian veteran, the Sieur de Pont (called Pontgrave), were in charge of this expedition. The expedition arrived at Tadousac without difficulty, and Champlain set off to select a suitable place at which to plan a trading post. It should be near enough to the sea for easy access from France and also near the northward-flowing tributaries of the St. Lawrence so that furs from the interior might be brought down by canoe.

Sailing upriver from Tadousac on the last day of June, Champlain decided to plant his post at a spot where a point of land jutted out into the river, narrowing the channel. Overhead high bluffs towered. Arriving at this spot on July 3, Champlain set his party to felling trees to build a stockade and cabins.

He wrote to his superiors in France: "Where I searched for a place suitable for our settlement, I could find none more convenient or better suited than the point of Quebec, so called by the Indians because it is covered with nut trees."

After the construction of the post, Pontgrave sailed back to France for the winter, leaving Champlain with 27 men to man the post. Among those who remained with Champlain were Nicholas Marsolet, Etienne Brule, a doctor named Bonnerme, Jean Duval, and Antoine Natel, a locksmith.

The winter was a hard one, and scurvy and dysentery claimed many victims. Natel died during the last of November, and some time after that the doctor, Bonnerme, also succumbed. There were 18 others attacked by scurvy, of whom 10 died. Five others were claimed by dysentery.

When the spring arrived, only eight of the 27 men were living, and Champlain himself was seriously ill. The French had not yet learned the need for fresh meat and had attempted to sustain themselves through the winter on ship's biscuit and salted meat.

With the arrival of spring came Claude Godet, Sieur de Marets, who was the son-in-law of Pontgrave. De Marets reported that Pontgrave was in Tadousac. Champlain then went to Tadousac himself, where he was handed a letter from de Monts, which asked that Champlain return to France to report on the progress of the post at Quebec and the progress of the fur trade.

Back in Quebec in September, Champlain then met Pontgrave at Tadousac, and the two sailed to France to report to de Monts. The latter, meanwhile, had been unable to get his fur trading monopoly extended. Crown officials decided to permit any French subject who wished to to engage in the fur trade.

De Monts, crestfallen at this, decided to withdraw from the venture since he saw no chance to make a profit under the changed conditions. De Monts' former partners, Collier and Legendre of Rouen, decided to continue the venture, and outfitted two ships at their own expense, which they placed under Pontgrave's command.

No provisions were made for Champlain to accompany this expedition, but he complained to de Monts, and the latter asked his partners to allow Champlain to sail with the expedition. This they agreed to, and in 1610, the new expedition sailed from Honfleur.

❝ The tireless Champlain, who possessed the temperament of one of the great explorers, spent much of his time in the New World in exploring the many waterways that entered upon the Great Lakes and the St. Lawrence River.❞

The tireless Champlain, who possessed the temperament of one of the great explorers, spent much of his time in the New World in exploring the many waterways that entered upon the Great Lakes and the St. Lawrence River.

In 1611, he led a small expedition up the St. Lawrence to the falls of the river. In 1613, he sought to find the fabled Northwest Passage by exploring the Ottawa River.

Throughout his career in New France, Champlain sought to strengthen the settlement at Quebec, develop the fur trade in the St. Lawrence River Valley, and maintain good relations with all of the northern tribes so that their furs would be brought to the trading post there and at Montreal.

In 1628, when war broke out between the French and the English—again—the English sent a naval squadron commanded by Capt. David Kirke to oust the French from the St. Lawrence.

When the English squadron suddenly arrived at Quebec, Champlain had only 18 men at the post. There was little to do but surrender, which Champlain did on Aug. 9, 1629.

Because of the poor communications of those days, neither Champlain nor Kirke realized that a treaty of peace had been signed between their two countries the previous April.

When the French government received word of the capture of Quebec, therefore, the return of the post was demanded. King Charles agreed, and Quebec was turned over to France once more, although it was not until 1632 that the French were able to take possession of the post again.

Champlain once more was sent back to the New World. There were only a few settlers on hand to greet the veteran, now 66, when he landed once more at Quebec. New houses were being built, along with a chapel, a convent and a school .

Champlain died on Christmas Day in 1635. Where he was buried has remained a mystery, but there is little doubt that without his skill and daring and his efficient administration the little colony at Quebec would have experienced much harder times and Canada might not have remained French.

CHAPTER 11

Warlike Iroquois trade furs for guns

During the years following the death of Champlain, events of major importance to the history of French America were taking place south of the St. Lawrence.

The Dutch, after "buying" Manhattan Island from a group of Indians who didn't own it, set up a series of trading posts along the Hudson River, hoping to gain a part of the fur trade for themselves.

It was not long before the men of the Iroquois Confederacy decided they would have this fur trade with the Dutch for their very own, and the native tribes in the lower New York regions were exterminated, or driven out.

The Iroquois quickly developed an appetite for European goods, especially for guns. In 1623, they traded more than 8,000 pelts to the Dutch, and by 1633 they were bringing in more than 30,000 pelts a year. Trade of such magnitude, of course, soon exhausted the supply of fur-bearing animals in Iroquois country.

The men of the confederacy, now dependent on European goods to maintain their improved standards of living, sought to obtain furs from the Algonquins and the Hurons, but these tribes were trading with the French. Thereupon, the Iroquois conceived a brilliant plan: having armed themselves with the white man's guns, they would take the war path against the northern tribes.

Their aim was simply extermination—the first recorded instance of attempted genocide in American history. The Iroquois reasoned that if the Hurons and the Algonquins, along with neighboring tribes, were eliminated, the Long House could control the fur trade of the whole Great Lakes-St. Lawrence region. Then they could direct the flow of furs to the French or the Dutch, as they pleased.

As early as 1633 a war party of the Long House attacked a party of Champlain's men on the St. Lawrence, killing two and wounding four others.

The French retaliated by extending their forts and posts farther up the river, and by sending missionaries to attempt to convert the native tribes. In 1634, a fort was built at Trois Rivières, at the juncture of the St. Lawrence and the St. Maurice rivers, one of the main river routes to the North.

In 1638, Jean Nicolet, an agent of the Company of New France, which was the commercial firm that "owned" the colony, penetrated the wilderness to Lake Michigan, then down Green Bay to the Fox River to establish trade relations with the Winnebagos, and to make peace between them and the Hurons. This opened up a vast new territory to the French fur trade.

Religious societies also played a major role in the expansion of the colony, both by supplying manpower and by supplying funds. In 1630, the Duc de Vandadour, then viceroy of New France, organized the Compagnie de St. Sacrament to promote missionary activities among the Indians.

This society, made up of men of great piety, wealth and influence in France, gave its support in 1640 to attempts to found a settlement at Montreal for the purpose of converting the neighboring Indians to Christianity.

Thus, Montreal can lay claim to being the only great metropolis in North America founded for purely religious purposes.

Some 50 devout colonists, therefore, established Ville Marie de Montreal, under the command of Paul de Chomeday, Sieur de Maisonneuve, a 33-year-old army veteran whose piety had greatly impressed the members of the founding society.

❢ *The Iroquois quickly developed an appetite for European goods, especially for guns. In 1623, they traded more than 8,000 pelts to the Dutch, and by 1633 they were bringing in more than 30,000 pelts a year.* ❣

Thus was the flag of France pushed to the juncture of the St. Lawrence and Ottawa rivers. Although the new post was ideally situated for the missionaries to gain access to the Indian tribes, it soon proved to be commercially important, too.

The Ottawa River was the principal route by which the Algonquins and the Hurons brought their furs to the French. A trading post at Montreal would save them the long paddle to Trois Rivières of Quebec, and possible ambush by the Iroquois along the way. It was not long, therefore, before trading facilities were established at Montreal, much to the dismay of the pious founders.

Since the settlement was made on territory claimed by the Iroquois, it is surprising that the small company was not attacked. The Iroquois overlooked the new colony, though, since their war parties were concentrated against the Hurons along Georgian Bay and the Ottawa.

CHAPTER 12

The advent
of the
coureurs de bois

Individual Frenchmen were not slow to venture into the wilds themselves, to meet tribesmen on the way to Quebec or Trois Rivières or Montreal, and to short-circuit the official trading posts. The natives would as soon trade with an individual in the forests as at a trading post, especially if he were thereby saved a long journey.

This tendency gave rise to the *coureur de bois,* a sort of backwoodsman who came to be the despair of French officialdom. They were a wild, unruly lot, and made themselves more obnoxious by trading whiskey to the Indians.

The prototype of this sort of backwoodsman was Etienne Brule, who came to Canada as Champlain's servant. He found an affinity for the forests, and soon deserted Quebec settlement. Thereafter, when he came to Quebec, he was always in Indian attire. He was said to be unusually strong, and was quick to learn Indian ways and Indian languages.

By 1680, authorities at Quebec estimated that between 800 and 1,000 Frenchmen were off in the forests illegally, seeking furs from the natives.

The life of the *coureur de bois* was not one for weaklings. It was hard and exacting. He was called upon to crouch in a narrow canoe and paddle hour after hour from dawn to dark, at 45 to 50 strokes per minute. For more than 1,000 miles the *coureurs* traveled thus, pulling their canoes through small rapids by ropes as they waded up to the waist in some swift and uncharted river, or carrying canoes and cargo on their shoulders to portage around great rapids.

The advent of the *coureurs de bois* marked a new tack in French relations with the Indians and began a headlong race between missionaries and traders to see if the former could convert the tribes to civilized ways before the traders destroyed them with whiskey and European diseases.

CHAPTER 13

Europeans pulled into Indian tribal warfare

The white man in the New World has often been censured for involving the Indian tribes in Europe's fratricidal warfares, making them but pawns in the hands of the empire builders.

In retrospect, however, it would be more accurate to say that the Indians involved the white men in their own inter-tribal warfare, and thus helped to intensify economic rivalries between the French, English, Dutch, Spanish and other colonists and traders who came to the New World.

When Samuel de Champlain, for example, made his voyage to the St. Lawrence River Valley in 1603, the first request made of him by the Algonquin and Montagnais tribes whom he visited was that he help them in their wars. Being the diplomat that he was, Champlain promised to do so when the time was ripe.

On his second voyage to Canada, in 1608, the same demands were made. The French wished to trade for the Algonquin and Montagnais furs? Very well, they should have no qualms about helping their red brothers strike a hard blow against their traditional enemies to the south. Otherwise, there might be few furs for the French to carry back home.

It was unfortunate that the time and the place of France's colonial efforts (and those of England later) would land the colonists in the middle of a century-old Indian war of extreme bitterness.

The reason for this was the rise of the Long House, better known as the Iroquois Confederacy.

Archeologists believe that the various tribes and clans which became the Iroquois originated in the southern Mississippi Valley in the era of the mound-builders. About the beginning of the Christian era they began a long migration northward, and by the Fourteenth Century seem to have established themselves in what is now New York state, west of the Hudson River.

There were five groups of these Indians, which the white men called tribes. The farthest east were the Keniengehagas or "flint people," called Mohawks, or "eaters of men," by their Algonquin enemies, indicating that they were—ceremonially, at least—cannibals. Then came the Goyo-gouins, whom the English called Cayugas; the Onontagues, or Onondagas; the Onneyouts, or Oneidas; and the Tsonnontouans, called Senecas by the English.

Through most of their history, these tribes were engaged in blood feuds and wars. War was self-perpetuating, since every death had to be avenged, and it might be said that the Iroquois looked upon war as the natural vocation of man.

Some time after their arrival in New York, probably between 1475 and 1500, two prophets sprang up among them—Hiawatha, a Mohawk, and Degandawida, a Huron adopted by the Onondaga. They persuaded the five tribes to bury the hatchet, to halt their wars and blood feuds, and to live together in peace.

This did not mean they gave up their warlike pursuits. They simply directed them against tribes outside the confederacy. After their confederation, they called themselves Ongwanosioni, or "People of the Long House," in honor of their elongated bark huts.

The Algonquins, who knew them too well from their long wars, called them Iriakhowi, or "true rattlesnakes."

The People of the Long House had a complex social system with a wide

❢ It was unfortunate that the time and the place of France's colonial efforts (and those of England later) would land the colonists in the middle of a century-old Indian war of extreme bitterness. ❢

> *An early, unknown contact with Christians had left the Iroquois with a legend of a flood, the prophecy of a savior and a confessional, and a distinct understanding of the role of the unconscious and dreams.*

variety of taboos, a highly developed religion, and an extensive, unwritten "literature." An early, unknown contact with Christians had left them with a legend of a flood, the prophecy of a savior and a confessional, and a distinct understanding of the role of the unconscious and dreams.

They were also among the cruelest, most bloodthirsty and most ruthless of peoples.

Because they could concentrate armies of several hundred, up to perhaps 2,000 warriors, the Iroquois brought a new and more deadly dimension to forest warfare, which previously had been a matter of raids and counterraids of a score or a few dozen combatants.

The Iroquois soon drove all other tribes from their area west of the Hudson and carried on a steadily escalating war with the Algonquins, the Hurons and the Montagnais to the north and to the west.

The Iroquois and their enemies had been in a major war in the St. Lawrence Valley since before the start of the Sixteenth Century. It was this ancient war in which Champlain was asked to participate when he visited his Indian friends near Three Rivers in 1608. In 1609, a gathering of Huron, Algonquin and Montagnais warriors gathered at Quebec and once more demanded that the French assist them in their wars. Champlain decided the politic thing to do was to accompany this force on its southern foray.

The party proceeded south, through Lake Champlain to Lake George, where they encountered an Iroquois force ready to fight. The fight opened, and arrows began to fly. Champlain was escorted to the front and fired his musket, which was loaded with four balls. Two of the Iroquois were killed and one was wounded, but the loud noise created more confusion among the Iroquois ranks. The Iroquois took flight and found shelter in the woods.

Some historians blame Champlain's participation in this raid for the subsequent hostility of the Iroquois to the French, but it seems far-fetched to believe that conditions would have been different had he not taken part.

The French were few in number, and they depended upon their Indian neighbors to maintain their lodgement at Quebec. Hostile Indian neighbors would have made the early settlement untenable. Besides, as long as the French traded with the Hurons or the Algonquins or the Montagnais, who were the Iroquois' enemies, it seems far-fetched to believe that the Iroquois would ever have had a friendly feeling toward the French.

Even if the French had maintained the strictest neutrality, it seems impossible that they might have avoided a confrontation with the restless and expansionist Iroquois, who seemed determined to subdue all of the forest tribes to their fierce will.

At any rate, the presence of the Iroquois in western New York meant that French colonization in that direction was blocked. This fact deflected French fur traders to the west, and eventually to the discovery of the Mississippi River and the planting of the French flag in what is now Louisiana.

CHAPTER 14

Converting the red man to Christianity

French efforts to convert the Indian tribes to Christianity date from the beginnings of the colony at Quebec. On his third voyage, Champlain brought with him four Franciscans of the Strict Observance, commonly known as Recollets.

They were Fathers Joseph le Caron, Jean d'Obleau, Denis Jamay and Pacifique du Plessis. The bishops of Paris subscribed a sum of 1,500 livres to cover the expenses of the mission, since the Recollets were a mendicant order, depending upon charity for their daily bread and the patched grey robes they wore.

The first Mass ever heard in Canada was celebrated by du Plessis. The four friars cut the trees, hewed the logs and carved the stone for their mission, a log building, surrounded by a palisade.

The vast program of converting thousands of savages, however, was beyond the resources of the Recollets, and in 1626 five members of the Society of Jesus were sent out to help them. Three were priests—Charles Lalemant, Jean de Brebeuf and Enemond Masse. Two were brothers of the order—François Charton and Gilbert Burel. Father Lalemant was appointed director of the Jesuit missionary effort.

The Recollets left the colony when it was captured by the English in 1629 and did not return when Quebec was restored to France by the Treaty of 1632. Thus, the Jesuits were left alone in the mission field.

Their numbers were considerably increased after 1632, principally due to the financial backing by pious members of the French court. They established missions among the Montagnais on the north shore of the Gulf of St. Lawrence, another at Miscou at the mouth of the Baie de Chaleur, and a third on Cape Breton.

In 1634, the Jesuits expanded their missionary efforts into the land of the Hurons east of Georgian Bay. Missions were established in the Huron villages of Ihonatiria and Ossossane, and in 1639 a third was established at the mouth of the Wye River. It was called Ste. Marie.

Ste. Marie consisted of a chapel, hospital, mill, stables, barns, a residence for the priests and another for lay workers, all surrounded by a log palisade. As many as 35 Frenchmen resided there from time to time— priests, lay brothers, agricultural workers, a surgeon, a druggist, a carpenter and other artisans.

The priests were seldom in residence, spending most of their time serving missions in outlying villages, or traveling by canoe to the distant Petun tribe, called the "Tobacco Nation" by the French, to the "Neutral" tribes to the southwest and to the Algonquins farther north.

These outposts, separated from the settlements on the St. Lawrence by thousands of miles, formed tiny islands of Baroque civilization in a Stone Age ocean.

The life of the missionaries was hard and demanding. Indian food was hard on European stomachs, and some of the Indian customs were revolting. The Indians existed on two meals a day, composed of corn ground between two stones and boiled into a mush. Mixed in with it were any dirt or insects which might have happened to be on the stones. If fish or birds were caught, they were thrown into the pot without being cleaned.

If a war party returning home with prisoners ran short of food, one of the captives was knocked in the head, butchered, and his flesh added to the community kettle.

Village life was not much better. Men, women, children and dogs with their fleas all crowded into the huts, winter and summer. There was little room to move, and in the center a fire filled the cramped space with smoke.

The difficulties of mastering Indian languages and dialects and of finding some way to communicate the rudiments of Christianity to these savages complicated the missionaries' task further.

Despite all of the difficulties, the Hurons offered the missionaries their best opportunity to make significant progress in Christianizing the savages. They were a relatively nonmigratory people, they practiced the rudiments of agriculture, and their villages were concentrated into a relatively compact area.

There were some 15,000 to 20,000 of them when French traders first made contact with them. The Hurons welcomed the missionaries among them and willingly listened to their sermons.

Many of them responded readily to Christian teachings, and baptisms were frequent. By the late 1640s, several thousand Hurons had accepted baptism. Hope was high in the minds of the missionaries that the entire nation might eventually accept the faith.

Father Isaac Jogues, S.J.
Missionary and martyr

The French also attempted to send missionaries to the Iroquois, but these attempts met with anything but success. The Rev. Isaac Jogues, for example, was captured and tortured by Iroquois in 1643 as he and two lay brothers and 17 Huron converts were paddling up the St. Lawrence River. The party was ambushed by 70 Iroquois. Most of the Hurons were killed and the three Frenchmen were captured. Father Jogues and his companions were stripped of their clothing and had their fingernails pulled out. Jogues was beaten senseless with war clubs. The three were forced to run the gauntlet and were beaten by Iroquois braves until they were drenched with blood and half dead. The Frenchmen got no sleep at night because the younger warriors pulled out their hair and beards. The village children amused themselves by placing live coals and red hot ashes on the bodies

❝ *The Hurons welcomed the missionaries among them and willingly listened to their sermons. Many of them responded readily to Christian teachings, and baptisms were frequent.* ❞

of the prisoners. The priest finally escaped and found refuge with the Dutch at Oswego, from whence he was able to return to France. One of the lay brothers also escaped, while the other gained the respect of a Mohawk brave and was adopted into the tribe.

Jogues was received with jubilation at Jesuit headquarters in Paris, and his reports were listened to eagerly. As for Jogues himself, he was already making plans to return to the Iroquois country and set up a mission post in their midst.

The savage killings of Jesuit priests and innocent converts

Throughout 1643 and 1644, the border warfare between the Iroquois and the Hurons, the Algonquins and the French continued. Losses were heavy on both sides, and neither gained an advantage.

In 1645, the Iroquois decided to ask for peace, and sent delegates to meet the French and their allies at Trois Rivières and bury the hatchet. Thus, the frontier had a short respite.

In 1645, too, the Rev. Isaac Jogues was back in Canada, and with the advent of peace was making plans for the foundation of a mission to the Iroquois, which he called "The Mission of the Martyrs."

In the middle of May he departed from Trois Rivières with an Algonquin escort, traveled to Fort Orange on the Hudson, where they were entertained by Dutch traders, and then departed for the Iroquois country.

Soon after the departure, the escort deserted, leaving Jogues and a lay brother, known to us only as Lalande. Soon, they were ambushed and captured by a Mohawk band and carried in triumph to the nearest Mohawk village.

Here crowds surrounded them, beating them savagely. A Mohawk cut strips of flesh from Jogues' back and legs, saying as he did so, "Let us see if this is the flesh of a great wizard."

In the evening, Jogues sat fainting from his wounds when he was summoned to the chief's hut. As he bent to enter, a Mohawk struck him from behind, sinking a tomahawk into the missionary's brain. Jogues fell at the feet of his murderer, who finished the job of hacking off his head. The next morning, Lalande suffered a like fate.

Jogues' fate was learned by the French from the Dutch at Fort Orange, who learned it from the Iroquois themselves .

The French missions prospered in the Huron country, but in the 1630s,

North American Indians discuss the fate of a white prisoner.

smallpox was introduced into the tribe by French traders. By the winter of 1645, more than half of the 15,000 Hurons had died from the disease.

No sooner had this plague abated than a new whirlwind struck. After three years of peace had recouped their forces, and after they had stocked up with guns from the Dutch, the Iroquois launched their blitzkrieg against the Hurons.

Without warning, the Iroquois columns debouched from the forests and attacked the Huron villages near St. Joseph Mission. Many of the Huron warriors were away on a hunt. Rushing the palisades at sunrise, the Iroquois soon hacked a path into the village. Within there was terror and panic at the first sound of the Long House war cries. The few warriors who tried to make a stand were shot down. Nor were the women and children spared. At the mission, the Rev. Antoine Daniel was celebrating Mass. He hurriedly baptized those he could before the Iroquois attacked the chapel. Then, in his white alb and red stole, and carrying a cross in front of him, Father Daniel went to the entrance. He was shot down at the chapel door, and the Iroquois swarmed around him. His body was stripped, his head hacked off, and his body gashed.

The neighboring village was served in a similar manner. Of the 3,000 people living in the two villages, only a few escaped. Some 700 were taken as prisoners and were subjected to torture and death in the Iroquois towns.

Though the rest of the summer passed with only sporadic attacks by the Iroquois, the Hurons lived in constant fear of the future attacks which they knew would be coming.

The next blow fell on March 16 of 1649, a grim and bloody year. The ice had not yet broken up and snow was thick on the ground when the Iroquois suddenly struck at a Huron village called St. Ignace. They had scaled the wall before dawn, when most of the village was sleeping. The slaughter was the same as before. Then the Iroquois tide flowed to the small mission chapel of St. Louis, manned by 80 Hurons and two priests, the Rev. Jean de Brebeuf and the Rev. Gabriel Lalemant. The Iroquois, a thousand strong, soon swarmed over the walls and put the Hurons to death. The two priests busily attended the wounded. Unfortunately for

---

❝ *After three years of peace had recouped their forces, and after they had stocked up with guns from the Dutch, the Iroquois launched their blitzkrieg against the Hurons.* ❞

---

them, they were not killed, but were captured and led away to torture.

The Iroquois stripped the two priests, tied them to a pole, tore out their fingernails and clubbed them all over their bodies. One of the Iroquois, who knew a smattering of French, told Brebeuf: "You say Baptism and suffering will lead to Paradise. You will go there soon, for I am going to baptise you." Then he proceeded to pour boiling water over the priest three times. Red-hot tomahawks were applied to his armpits and stomach.

Through the torture, Brebeuf continued to preach to the Iroquois, urging them to forsake their paganism and accept Christianity. Not wanting to hear him speak, they cut out his tongue and cut off his lips. Then they stripped the flesh from his legs, roasted it and ate it. He was scalped, and his heart was torn out, roasted and eaten. Some of the Indians drank his still-warm blood.

Father Lalemant was put through a similar ordeal.

The remains of the two priests were found a few days later by other missionaries and were brought to Quebec for burial.

CHAPTER 15

Iroquois make and break the peace – again

The two great raids by the Iroquois on the Huron villages terrorized the remaining villages. And even after the Iroquois armies had retired, the death toll among the Hurons continued to rise.

Some 15 outlying villages were deserted, and the refugees flocked to the French mission at Ste. Marie. More than 6,000 disconsolate Hurons huddled around the stone church. The missionaries did all they could to feed the multitude, but starvation threatened them all. The Hurons' food supplies had gone up in the smoke of their villages.

The Iroquois soon moved against Ste. Marie, but here a Huron counterattack drove them off. The Iroquois army retired to St. Ignace, amused itself with burning its prisoners for a while, and then retired to Iroquois country, carrying a rich harvest of scalps and furs.

The Hurons' will to resist was by now broken, and there seemed nothing to do for the survivors but to flee. They simply could not stand against the Iroquois and their guns. Some sought refuge with the Neutral nation, others with the Petun, the Erie and the Ottawa.

By summer the Huron nation was no more. Only piles of ashes, charred human bones and clearings in the forest where vast corn fields had once been planted remained to mark the existence of this once-powerful and populous tribe .

The destruction of the Hurons forced the French missionaries—and traders—to extend their efforts to tribes farther into the interior of the continent. Meanwhile, the Iroquois launched further wars against the Erie and the Neutral tribes, but permanent victory eluded them. They were operating too far from their base and lacked the sophisticated system of supply to keep them for long in enemy country.

In 1653, the Iroquois again sought peace with the French, convinced that the destruction of the Hurons would allow the Iroquois to take charge of the fur trade. Peace was agreed upon, and the Iroquois were free to trade with either the French or the Dutch.

Meanwhile, the French were setting up relations with more western tribes. French fur traders were voyaging to the western Great Lakes to trade with the "far Indians." By 1656 many voyagers, including Pierre Esprit Radisson and Medart Chouart de Groseilliers, had established relations with far western tribes.

On these voyages they began to hear rumors of a great river that ran south to the Great Southern Sea, which in turn washed the shores of the Indes.

After being interrupted only a few years, the flow of furs once again began to reach Montreal and Trois Rivières. None of the furs came in Iroquois canoes, however, because the Ottawas of the Northwest had stepped in to take the place of the Hurons.

The Iroquois were furious. All of their long campaigns had gained them nothing. Once more they took to the warpath and began blockading the rivers leading into the St. Lawrence Valley, stopping the fur trade from the west once more.

When the settlers went out in the morning to tend their crops or livestock, they could never be sure of seeing their families again at the end of the day. In the field, behind any stump, tree, stone or hill a Mohawk could conceal himself, waiting patiently for hours until the settler came within range of his gun or tomahawk.

War parties of 100 or more ravaged settlements from Montreal to Quebec, destroying crops, burning homes and barns, and slaughtering stragglers.

Finally, in 1663, the authorities at Quebec applied for aid from the French government at home. France, at the time under the able direction of Jean-Baptiste Colbert, had the most efficient government in Europe. Colbert had an important task for Canada, since he wanted it to supply the mother country with timber, ship masts and naval stores, as well as furs.

Colbert decided to revise the government of the colony. He canceled the

> **To make the colony more secure from the Iroquois, the Carignan Salières regiment of the French army was shipped to Quebec, comprising nearly 1,100 men under veteran officers.**

charter of the commercial company that had ruled Canada and made it a crown colony. To make the colony more secure from the Iroquois, the Carignan Salières regiment of the French army was shipped to Quebec, comprising nearly 1,100 men under veteran officers.

In the fall of 1666, the regiment, plus 400 Canadian militia, led by the newly appointed viceroy, Alexandre de Prouville, Sieur de Tracy, invaded the Mohawk country.

The Mohawks declined to fight and faded into the forest depths. The French burned their four villages, containing all their winter food supplies, and then marched back to Quebec. No Mohawks were killed or captured, but the loss of food supplies was a severe blow. Also severe was the loss of huts, furs, canoes and other equipment that was extremely hard to replace.

In fact, it was a hard year for the Long House. A Mohawk and Onendaga war party had been almost annihilated by the Ottawas, and the Seneca and the Cayuga had been mauled by the Andastes. The Iroquois had spread themselves too thin in their wars of conquest. In addition, smallpox swept through the Long House villages, probably contracted during their wars against the Hurons. Faced with these disasters and expecting more French expeditions, the Long House decided once more to sue for peace.

An Iroquois delegation appeared before Quebec, and accepted the terms profferred by Viceroy Tracy. They agreed to halt their wars against the French and all of their Indian allies.

With peace in both Canada and Europe, the way was open for a further development of the colony and a serious colonization effort on the part of Colbert. The officers and men of the Carignan Salières regiment, who had been sent to Canada with the understanding that they would be returned to France after 18 months, were given every encouragement to remain as settlers.

Several officers and men—some 400 in number—agreed to remain, and were given land grants. It was an important reinforcement for the colony. In addition, peaceful conditions and improved administration enabled the French to concentrate upon extending their influence farther into the interior.

CHAPTER 16

Adventures in westward expansion

The fur trade was the mainstay of French Canada. From its revenues came the money to maintain the colony. It was the first business of the colony, therefore, to see that the fur trade flourished.

This meant, inevitably, that the French must penetrate farther and farther into the interior, since the trade on the scale as it was being carried out soon exhausted the supply of wildlife in a given territory, forcing a westward expansion.

The westward expansion had other impulses, too. There were tales of copper mines in the interior and stories of the great river that perhaps flowed into the shores of the Great Sea by the cities of Cathay.

The Jesuits were in the forefront of the westward thrust. Father Claude Dablon conducted a mission at Ste. Marie du Sault, in a square enclosure of cedar logs, with a hut and a chapel. At the other end of Lake Superior, another young Jesuit, the Rev. Jacques Marquette, had charge of the Mission de St. Esprit at La Pointe.

Thence came Louis Joliet, appointed by the authorities in Quebec to hunt for copper mines. Another pioneer in westward explorations was Daniel Greysolon, Sieur du L'Hut, whose main achievement was opening

> *Marquette and Joliet came to a place of unusual beauty, where the Wisconsin River, which they had been following, joined a new and wide stream which rolled majestically toward the south. Their Indian guides assured them with gestures and much eloquent oratory that this was indeed the great Father of Waters.*

up the country west and south of Lake Superior.

In 1680, with a party of four Frenchmen and an Indian guide, he spied out the lay of the land around the Brule and St. Croix rivers. He established a trading post at the mouth of the St. Louis River, and in years to come this was to grow into the city of Duluth, named in his honor.

The Jesuits knew that beyond Green Bay were regions where buffalo roamed by the thousands, and there were tribes who had never heard the Gospel. They also heard the stories of the great river that flowed into the South Sea and decided to send an expedition to find it.

For this purpose they chose Louis Joliet, who had already been exploring in the west looking for copper mines. To accompany the experienced Joliet, they chose one of their own number, the Rev. Jacques Marquette.

They set out for the west on May 17, 1672, in two canoes with five companions. En route they encountered many new and strange tribes—the Wild-Rice Indians, the Miamis, Mascoutins and Kickapoos.

Then one day, about a month after their start, they came to a place of unusual beauty, where the Wisconsin River, which they had been following, joined a new and wide stream which rolled majestically toward the south.

Their Indian guides assured them with gestures and much eloquent oratory that this was indeed the great Father of Waters, the Mechezebbet, which flowed for thousands of miles into the Great South Sea.

The Indians were awed by it, and urged the French to go no farther upon its broad surface. Huge monsters, that made a habit of eating men, besieged the southern reaches of the river, they said. This was probably the first mention that the French had of Louisiana alligators.

Marquette and Joliet were not to be dissuaded, however, and followed the great river south until they reached the mouth of the Arkansas. At that point they decided to turn back. They knew not how many more hundreds of miles the river flowed, but they were now sure that it flowed into the Gulf of Mexico, rather than the Vermilion or the Great South Sea.

Now the way was cleared for further French penetration of the interior.

Father Jacques Marquette, Jesuit priest and famous explorer, holds up a symbol of peace as he approaches unknown Indians in an unexplored region along the northern Mississippi River. While the French and other European pioneers generally didn't understand the Indians' languages – and vice versa – the peace pipe was a universally recognized symbol which meant "We come in peace; we mean you no harm."

Part III

LaSalle and the Father of Waters

René Robert Cavalier, Sieur de la Salle is the most famous of the French explorers. He traveled from the St. Lawrence River and down the Mississippi all the way to the Gulf of Mexico – and was the first man known to do so. He claimed the heartland of the continent for France in April of 1682.

CHAPTER 17

The great explorer begins his quest

In 1667 there appeared on the Canadian scene one of the chief actors in the great drama that would win for France an inland empire almost beyond measure. René Robert Cavalier, Sieur de la Salle, was born at Rouen of a noble and wealthy family.

In his early youth he resolved to join the Jesuit order and fit himself for the mission fields of the New World. He entered the Jesuit novitiate at the age of 15 and progressed far enough to win the title of "scholastic" and to be sent to teach in a Jesuit school at Alençon, being later transferred to Tours and then to Blois.

LaSalle was not successful as a teacher, being too impatient with his pupils. In fact, he found the teaching profession a boring one, and was much too active in body and mind for the classroom.

Finally, LaSalle asked to be sent at once to take up his work in the missions, but it was judged that his spiritual training had not proceeded far enough. With this setback, LaSalle asked for his release from the order, and at the age of 24 his resignation was accepted.

Finding himself free, and with little to maintain him in France, LaSalle took a ship to Canada. He arrived during the summer of 1667 and joined an older brother, who was a member of the Sulpician Order, in Montreal.

The younger LaSalle won the friendship of the Sulpicians, and they made him a grant of land on Montreal Island, where they were attempting to develop a series of farms. This was a wide and valuable domain, and LaSalle immediately cut it into farms, and set about attracting tenants.

He cleared some of the land for himself, built a house on it, and still found time to study Indian languages. Almost from the beginning, however, LaSalle's mind was not upon his farm, but upon the Great West that lay beyond the view of French voyageurs.

One winter a group of Indians from the Seneca tribe camped on his land, and the tales they told were so interesting LaSalle invited them to spend the winter. They told him of the "Beautiful River," running due west, which was larger even than the St. Lawrence, and which finally emptied into the Vermilion Sea.

These exotic names fired LaSalle's imagination. The Vermilion Sea could only mean the warm seas of the Orient! LaSalle was determined to find this great river and follow it to its mouth. He informed the Sulpician Fathers, and found them sympathetic. They arranged to buy back all of his land except the plot he had laid out for himself. This gave him enough money to outfit an expedition, and he decided to join a mission that the Sulpicians were sending to the Shawnee Indians. The party of 14 set out in four canoes on July 6, 1669. They were retained a month at one of the Seneca villages, but then crossed the Niagara River, hearing the roar of the great falls in the distance.

By the end of September, they reached an Indian village at the site of what is now Hamilton, Ontario. Here LaSalle parted company with the Sulpicians and headed his canoes south. He was not heard from for two years.

Just where he went is a matter of debate, but he almost certainly reached the "Beautiful River," now called the Ohio. He followed it downstream to a waterfall, which he described as "fort haut," and which blocked further progress. This was probably the falls above Louisville.

One of the staunchest of the supporters of the Sieur de LaSalle during his explorations of the western areas of New France was the new governor of the province.

Louis de Buade, Comte de Frontenac et de Palluau, succeeded Rémy de Courcelle as governor and lieutenant general of New France, and arrived in Quebec on Sept. 12, 1672.

He immediately set upon a policy of vigorous expansion of colonial activities, particularly in the realm of the fur trade. One of Frontenac's first projects was the erection of a French fort on Lake Ontario to hold the Iroquois in check and to intercept the fur trade that the western tribes were carrying on with the Dutch and English in New York.

Frontenac early made the acquaintance of LaSalle, and consulted with the young explorer and fur trader often. LaSalle was a student of the Iroquois and knew a great deal about the western country. He supplied the maps that convinced Frontenac that his fort should be built at Cataraqui, where Kingston, Ontario, now stands. It was to be called Fort Frontenac.

The fort was built in 1673, and the experience brought Frontenac and LaSalle to develop grander plans for trade and discovery. LaSalle burned with an ambition to secure the western country, and sought the governor's backing in a scheme to construct forts along the great river that Marquette and Joliet had discovered, and to build a greater empire than Canada for the French crown.

The next year, LaSalle went to France to seek financial backing for this great venture, and carried with him a letter of introduction to Colbert, the French minister of state. LaSalle made favorable impressions upon Colbert and other ministers, as well as the king.

His project was adopted. He was granted a patent of nobility on condition that he rebuild Fort Frontenac with stone and maintain its garrison at his own expense. In 1675, LaSalle was back in New France, where he rebuilt the fort as he had been directed, planted grain fields, established a mission school and built ships with which to navigate Lake Ontario in pursuit of the fur trade.

In 1677, LaSalle returned to France to gain permission of the king to lead an expedition to explore the great western river to its mouth. Again his petition was acted upon favorably.

Since he had no finances of his own lavish enough for such an undertaking, LaSalle induced a number of merchants, relatives and officials to advance him sums of money to undertake the exploration.

On July 14, 1678, LaSalle sailed from La Rochelle with 32 men, a supply of stores and implements for building ships on the great lakes and the great river. He reached Quebec two months later.

One of the men whose services he gained in Paris was destined to leave his name in history among the great explorers of the west. He was Henri di Tonti, an Italian by blood and a Frenchman by service.

There have been few more romantic spirits in American history. His exploits in the Mississippi Valley were the stuff of which legends are made. His indomitable energy overcame a weak physique. He endured privations that would have broken lesser men. He was at home in every environment, in the court of Louis XIV as easily as with the *coureurs de bois,* squaw men and renegades of the frontier.

He was the son of Lorenzo di Tonti, a banker who fled his native Naples after participating in an unsuccessful revolt. Lorenzo fled to France, where he became a financier and where he invented the form of lottery known as a "tontine."

His son entered a French military academy, served four years as a midshipman at Marseilles and Toulon and made seven military campaigns—four in ships and three in galleys. While he was serving in Sicily, his right hand was blown off by a grenade. He was captured and held prisoner for six months. Later he was released in an exchange of prisoners.

He returned to France, where the king granted him a pension for his heroism. He replaced his lost hand with one of iron, and later on the American frontier this awed his Indian friends, who dubbed him "Iron Hand." He was at Versailles when LaSalle came there, and they were introduced. LaSalle promptly enlisted Tonti's services for the expedition.

When LaSalle's expedition arrived at Fort Frontenac, the first task was to build a ship to sail the lakes. Tonti's experience was utilized and a sloop named "Le Griffon" was launched. On Aug. 7, LaSalle and his men embarked, entered Lake Huron, weathered a terrible storm and finally anchored at the Mission of St. Ignace, at the Straits of Mackinac.

Within a few days, LaSalle sailed into Green Bay, where he met some of his traders, and a huge store of pelts was taken aboard. On Sept. 18, LaSalle sent the ship back to Niagara with the cargo that would help to pay off some of his creditors.

LaSalle then took 18 men and set off along the western and southern shores of Lake Michigan toward the mouth of the St. Joseph River. Tonti and 20 men were dispatched by land along the eastern shores for the same destination. LaSalle arrived at the St. Joseph first, and set about building a fort there.

Three weeks passed and neither the ship nor Tonti appeared. Tonti finally arrived toward the end of November, but there was no word of the ship. Tonti had only half of his men. His provisions had failed, and he had been forced to leave half of his men 30 leagues behind to sustain themselves by hunting while he pushed on. Finally, all arrived, and LaSalle decided to push on before ice closed all the streams.

The party of 34 ascended the St. Joseph in eight canoes that often had to be dragged through the shallow, boulder-strewn and icy current. Near the present site of South Bend, Indiana, they made a portage to the Kankakee River, toiling through snow-mantled country and down narrow, twisting streams flowing through reedy and frozen marshes.

Finally they reached the point where the Kankakee and Des Plaines rivers join to form the Illinois. Gliding down the Illinois, past the tall cliffs of Starved Rock, they came to a large town of the Illinois Indians. The town was deserted, as the inhabitants were on a hunt, but on Christmas Day the French landed and took 30 bushels of maize from an underground storage basin for their provisions.

They pushed on through Peoria Lake. Just beyond they discovered an Indian village. They went ashore, and obtained more provisions when the Indians, members of the Illinois tribe, proved to be friendly.

Facing bitter winter weather that would make further exploration impossible, LaSalle decided to winter at the site. He built a small fort on a hill in what is now the suburbs of Peoria. He named it Fort Crèvecoeur, after the Dutch stronghold that the French under Marshal Turenne had captured in July of 1672. Tonti had served as one of Turenne's officers in that engagement.

In March 1680, with spring near, LaSalle decided to go back to Canada to seek word of "Le Griffon" and to secure more supplies for his expedition to the Mississippi. Five men were to accompany him, and Tonti was left with the others in command of the fort.

CHAPTER 18

LaSalle and Tonti push on despite sufferings and hardships

When LaSalle set out in March of 1680 to return from the Illinois country to Canada, he faced a long and dangerous journey. LaSalle had five companions—four Frenchmen and one Mohegan hunter. They traveled in two canoes, and set out on the long journey back to the fort that LaSalle had built at the mouth of the St. Joseph River.

Winter still gripped the land, and they were forced to drag their canoes over ice and through swift currents. Often they paddled in a cold rain that froze the clothes to their skins. They endured hunger and fatigue and all the other privations of the wilderness.

Finally they arrived at the fort on the St. Joseph River, where LaSalle had left two men to await "Le Griffon." They reported no news of the ship. There was nothing to do but go on to Niagara.

LaSalle left the canoes at the fort and led his party across the St. Joseph River on a raft. Then, by foot, they crossed southern Michigan, forcing their way through dense woods, choked with brambles and underbrush, eluding Iroquois hunting parties that ranged the forests.

At last they came to a stream which they followed to Lake Erie. Here they built another raft, crossed the Detroit River, and then resumed their long march across the northern shore of Lake Erie, through torrents of rain and flooded woods.

After much suffering they finally came to the French fort at Niagara on Easter Monday. Here LaSalle received the depressing news that "Le Griffon" had never arrived on its voyage from the fort on the St. Joseph. Her fate is still unknown. He also learned that another cargo ship had sunk at the mouth of the St. Lawrence River, carrying to the bottom a cargo valued at 22,000 livres which had been sent to him from France.

Disappointed, but not discouraged, LaSalle set out once more for Fort Frontenac, arriving there on May 6, after covering more than 1,000 miles in 65 days, much of it on foot.

His disappointments were not at an end, however. At Frontenac he found a letter from Tonti awaiting him. Tonti reported that the garrison at Fort Crèvecoeur had mutinied, torn down the fort's palisade and fled into the forest after throwing into the river all the arms and ammunition they could not carry. Tonti was left with five men, two of whom were missionaries.

LaSalle later learned that some of the mutineers were on the way to Fort Frontenac to murder him as the best way to escape punishment for their mutiny.

LaSalle sent out patrols, however, and when seven of the deserters appeared in two canoes, they were taken prisoner. The next day, the remainder were taken in the same way.

Undaunted by all of his ill fortune, LaSalle hurried his preparations to return to the Illinois country. He was fortunate in obtaining the services of François Daupin, Sieur de la Forest, with 25 men.

They traveled to Mackinac, where LaSalle left La Forest to gather stores and follow as soon as possible. With ten Frenchmen, two Indian hunters and a number of dogs, LaSalle pushed hurriedly onward. He reached the fort at the mouth of the St. Joseph and left five men there to await La Forest.

With the remaining men, he ascended the Kankakee and crossed to the site of the village of the Illinois. There they were greeted by sights of horror. The village had been burned and stakes thrust in the ground upon which were human skulls. Here and there crows and vultures tore the bodies of slain Illinois tribesmen, and wolves prowled through the village.

Cornfields had been burned or cut down. The ground was strewn with pots and kettles from the Illinois cellars, where they had kept their supplies and belongings. All of this was the work of the Iroquois, who had invaded the Illinois country and wiped out the tribe.

There were no signs of Tonti and the few loyal men who had remained with him. One by one LaSalle and his men examined the ghastly corpses, fearing to find that each one was French. But they were all Indians.

The French huddled in the darkness that night, keeping watch should the grim foe strike again.

The next day, they paddled farther down river on the way to Fort Crèvecoeur, passing ruined and deserted Illinois villages on the way. The fort was deserted and the surrounding country was a vast graveyard. Tied to stakes here and there were half-charred bodies of Illinois men, women and children. Day after day, they continued their search for Tonti and his men.

Beyond the junction of the Kankakee and Des Plaines rivers they stumbled across a cabin, where they saw a piece of wood that had recently been sawed. But they found nothing more.

It was now winter again, and LaSalle sadly turned his footsteps back to the fort on the St. Joseph. He left two men to guard the supplies and canoes and with the rest of the party set off on foot.

Snow fell for 19 days in succession, and the cold was so severe that LaSalle later wrote that he had never known a harder winter.

After much suffering, they arrived at the fort on the St. Joseph, where they found La Forest and the rest of the party, but no word from Tonti. LaSalle sought to throw off his despondency by making new plans. He sought to gain an alliance with a band of Abenaki and Mohegan Indians who had been driven from New England by the Puritans.

He also set out on a winter journey to visit the unmolested villages of the Illinois, to seek their support in his objective of exploring and settling the valley of the great river.

The glare of the snow gave LaSalle and some of the others snowblindness, and the party had to halt, near a camp of Fox Indians. The Foxes said they had seen six white men traveling from a village of the Potawatomi toward Green Bay. The six men had kept themselves alive on elderberries and wild onions, LaSalle was told.

LaSalle was convinced this was a report of Tonti and his men and that while he had come down the eastern shore of Lake Michigan, they had gone north along the opposite shore.

As soon as LaSalle had regained his sight, he returned to the fort on the St. Joseph, and then hurried up Lake Michigan to Mackinac. There he was overjoyed to meet Tonti, who had arrived from Green Bay the previous day.

Tonti revealed that he and his men had been captured by the Iroquois and condemned to death. An Onondaga chief, however, had interceded for them, and they had been released with a leaky canoe. On the way back, one of the missionaries, saying his breviary during a stop on shore, was killed by a Kickapoo war party.

Their leaky canoe was soon wrecked, and they were forced to walk. Tonti came down with fever, and suffered from swollen legs, but they staggered on. They sought help from the Potawatomi, but found the village deserted, and found little food.

Having worn out their shoes, they covered their feet with parts of the surviving missionary's cloak. In this strait, they were discovered by a band of Ottawas, who escorted them to another Potawatomi village, where they spent the rest of the winter, and in the spring they went on to Mackinac.

These adventures illustrate the hardships and sufferings which explorers and pathfinders were forced to endure in opening up the west.

CHAPTER 19

The Great Expedition

LaSalle was in a fever to make another attempt at exploring the Mississippi to its mouth, and hardly had he been reunited with Tonti than he began to plan his next expedition.

He was determined to streamline his operations and decided that the best course was to recruit a mixed group of French and Indians to make the long voyage to the south. He began to preach the need for a confederation of the Indian tribes who dwelt in the west. If they joined forces, they could defend themselves against the Iroquois.

He lobbied his ideas among the Miamis, Shawnees from the Ohio River Valley, Potawatamis from the west and Abenakis and Mohegans who had been exiled from New England by the English and the Iroquois.

The next step was to return to Quebec and put the idea of another expedition before Gov. Frontenac. LaSalle's plan was to employ a hard core of the most trustworthy Frenchmen he could find, teaming them with Indians who were at home in the forest wilds.

To raise money for this new venture, LaSalle sold parts of his fur monopolies and borrowed from his family in France. Then he and Tonti, having recruited their expedition, set off for the Illinois country and the first stages of one of the most important ventures ever undertaken in the New World.

The expedition consisted of 23 Frenchmen and 18 Abenaki and Mohegan Indians. As was their custom, the Indians brought along their wives and children. This made a large group, which some of the Frenchmen felt was too unwieldy.

LaSalle, however, knew what he was about. The Mohegans and the Abenakis were well-armed and expert in the use of their weapons. They were less likely to desert than the voyageurs, and they could be counted upon to do the bulk of the paddling, hunting and scouting.

The Indian women, LaSalle knew, would be expected to cook the food, do more than their fair share of portaging, do all the camp chores, live on scraps and free the Indians for the hunting and scouting.

On Dec. 31, 1681, the expedition arrived at Fort Miami. After a pause there, they set out toward the south, walking on the surface of the frozen Illinois River.

For 120 miles they trudged along on the ice. Then the ice began to break up, and they took to the shore, reloading the canoes, and launching them into the ice-filled stream.

They paddled down the Illinois, through the leafless forests, and then on Feb. 6 the expedition issued upon the broad surface of the great river itself.

Who were these men who were destined to be the first Europeans of record to set foot in Louisiana? LaSalle's journals yield their names. In addition to LaSalle and Tonti, there were Father Zénobe, a Recollet friar; the Sieur de Boisrondet; Jacques Bourdon, Sieur d'Autray; Jean Michel, surgeon; Jacques de Meterie, notary; Pierre Prud'homme, armorer.

Also, Jacques Cochois, Anthoine Bassard, Jean Masse, Pierre You, Colin Grevel, Jean de Lignon, André Henault, Gabriel Barbier, Pierre Mignaret, Nicolas de la Salle, André Boboeuf, Pierre Buret, Louis Baron, Jean Pignabel, and one individual merely designated as La Violette.

LaSalle's notary did not record the names of the Indians who made up such an important part of the expedition.

In relative comfort, the expedition paddled down the great river, uneventful day following uneventful day. One evening about dark they saw on their right the course of a great river and were awed at the rush of the muddy current of the Missouri entering the clear waters of the Mississippi. Later they passed the mouth of the Ohio, and on Feb. 24 camped on the heights of the Chickasaw Bluffs. They built a small stockade there, and LaSalle named it Fort Prud'homme.

Day after day they followed the river, until March 13 when in the midst of a thick fog, they heard on the right shore the booming of a war drum and the shrill whoops of Indians.

LaSalle ordered the canoes to keep near the far bank. Suddenly the fog

> € *LaSalle's plan was to employ a hard core of the most trustworthy Frenchmen he could find, teaming them with Indians who were at home in the forest wilds. He and Tonti, having recruited their expedition, set off for the Illinois country and the first stages of one of the most important ventures ever undertaken in the New World.* 9

lifted, and the Frenchmen saw an Indian town. The Indians were astonished at the sight of the white men, and after LaSalle displayed a peace pipe, the expedition landed at the town. They discovered it was a village of the Kappa (Quapaw) band of the Arkansas tribe, near the mouth of the Arkansas River.

After a feast and much celebration, the expedition set forth again, this time accompanied by two Kappa guides. They passed the mouth of the Arkansas, where Marquette and Joliet had turned back, and continued on past what is now Vicksburg and Grand Gulf.

About 300 miles below the Arkansas, the expedition halted on the edge of a vast swamp on the western shore of the river. Here, their two guides told them, lay the path to the great city of the Tensas. LaSalle decided to send Tonti and Friar Zénobe to visit this tribe. Thus, the two were probably the first white men to set foot in Louisiana, since the village was located in what is now Tensas Parish.

Tonti and Friar Zénobe, accompanied by native paddlers, carried their canoe through the swamp and launched it on a lake which had once formed part of the channel of the great river. In two hours they reached the town, and were astounded at its extent.

The houses were square structures built of mud and straw, with dome-shaped roofs made of cane.

There were two larger structures, one being the lodge of the chief and the other the House of the Sun, a temple. Tonti paid his respects to their chief, who sat on what appeared to be a bedstead, with three of his wives attending him, and surrounded by his council of 60 old men, clad in white cloaks made of mulberry bark.

When the chief spoke, his wives howled to do him honor, Tonti said, and his council gave him due reverence. When a chief died, Tonti was told, 100 men were sacrificed.

The chief received Tonti graciously, and later visited LaSalle. He was preceded by a master of ceremonies and six heralds, and when he arrived at the meeting place he was clad in a white robe and accompanied by two men bearing fans and a third with a huge copper disc representing the Sun, thought by the Tensas to be their chief's elder brother.

The interview was friendly, and the French departed the next morning, going downriver again, this time with Tensas guides.

CHAPTER 20

LaSalle claims
Louisiana for France

After their visit with the Tensas, the French explorers continued down the Mississippi. Now LaSalle and his men had entered the realms of eternal spring. The hazy sunlight filtered through the warm and drowsy air, which came from the banks of the river laden with the scent of a thousand exotic blossoms.

They saw extensive swamps and green canebrakes on both sides of the river, filled with thousands upon thousands of wildfowl. They heard for the first time the fearful bellow of the alligator, and some of the hunters killed a couple of these huge beasts.

One morning they happened upon a wooden dugout full of Indians, and Tonti gave chase as the dugout withdrew rapidly. As the dugout neared the bank, more than 100 Indians armed with bows and arrows appeared out of the canebrakes. LaSalle hastily called to Tonti to withdraw.

Tonti volunteered to return to the bank with a peace pipe to open negotiations. The Indians received them with signs and friendship, whereupon LaSalle and the remainder of the expedition followed. They proceeded to the village, where they spent the night.

These were the Natchez Indians, whose great chief dwelled in a large town near the present site of Natchez, Miss., and LaSalle and his men traveled to meet the great chief. There they found a village and a tribal hierarchy much like they had found among the Tensas.

The next day, LaSalle began the descent of the Mississippi anew, and two leagues below the Natchez they visited the Koroas, where they found another hearty welcome from the red men.

On March 31, the expedition passed a village of the Houma Indians, and that night camped just below the junction of the Red River and the Mississippi.

Three days later they surprised a fleet of wooden canoes, fishing in the canes along the edge of the water. The Indians fled at the sight of the Frenchmen. LaSalle sent a party to reconnoiter, but as they entered the marsh, the scouts were greeted with a volley of arrows.

In the surrounding forest, they heard the sound of drums and the whoops of mustering savages. Prudently, LaSalle recalled his scouts, and desiring to keep the peace along the river, resumed his course. The tribesmen probably belonged to the Quinipissas, who dwelt in what is now St. Charles Parish.

A few leagues below, the French came to a cluster of three villages on the left bank of the river, apparently devoid of inhabitants. LaSalle landed a party, and the three villages were found to be filled with corpses. These villages of the Tangipahoa tribe had been sacked by their enemies only a few days before.

By now, the French were nearing the end of their daring venture. On April 6, the expedition arrived at a place where the river divided itself into three branches.

LaSalle divided his party. He descended the westernmost branch. Tonti took the central passage, and the Sieur d'Autray descended the eastern arm. They moved through flat country, the current flowing sluggishly between the shores of reeds and marshes.

The water was brackish, and the horizon was limited on all sides by wind-driven walls of gray-brown reeds. The brackish water grew salty, and the breeze was fresh with the tang of the sea.

Then the reeds fell behind, and before LaSalle's canoe there rolled the broad, boundless surface of the Gulf of Mexico, tranquil, shimmering in the sun, without a sail, as unsullied as when it came forth from the bourne of time.

It must have been an exultant moment for LaSalle. Despite the hardships, the setbacks, the disappointments, this fierce, proud man had reached his goal. For the first time a white man had traveled from the St. Lawrence River to the Gulf of Mexico, through the heart of an unknown continent, traveling by water except for a few miles overland.

From his early days in Canada, LaSalle had searched for a great central waterway, and now he had proved that it existed.

It must have been an exultant moment for LaSalle. Despite the hardships, the setbacks, the disappointments, this fierce, proud man had reached his goal. For the first time a white man had traveled from the St. Lawrence River to the Gulf of Mexico, through the heart of an unknown continent, traveling by water except for a few miles overland.

LaSalle set his paddlers to work coasting the marshy borders of the sea before he decided to return to the rendezvous at the conjunction of the three distributaries. When all had reassembled, LaSalle held a ceremony claiming all of the surrounding lands for France.

A column was set up, bearing the rudely carved inscription: "Louis le Grand, Roy de France et Navarre, Règne; Le Neuvième Avril, 1682" (Louis the Great, King of France at Navarre, reigning; April 9, 1682). Beside the column, a large cross was erected. Beneath the cross LaSalle buried a leaden plate on which were scratched the words: "Ludovicus Magnus Regnat" (Louis the Great reigning).

Father Zénobe bestowed his blessing upon the party, and LaSalle formally proclaimed the land as the possession of France, giving to Louis XIV and his successors "the possession of this country of Louisiana, the seas, harbors, ports, bays, adjacent straits, and all the nations, peoples, provinces, cities, towns, villages, mines, minerals, fisheries, streams and rivers, within the extent of the said Louisiana, from the mouth of the great river and the rivers which discharge themselves thereinto, from its sources beyond the country of the Nadouessioux (the Sioux) and as far as its mouth at the sea, or the Gulf of Mexico."

With one magnificent gesture, LaSalle had presented to his sovereign the heart of an entire continent, an area many times larger than France, and named in honor of its new overlord.

Part IV

The Colonization of Louisiana

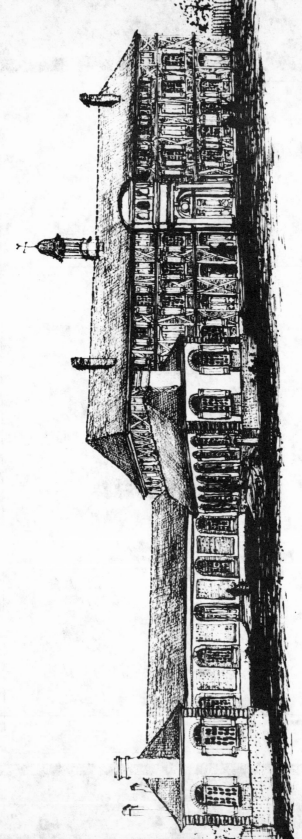

The Ursuline Convent in New Orleans, as it appeared in 1732. The convent housed not only the Ursuline Sisters, but also the filles a la cassette, who began arriving from France in 1722. Called "casket girls" because each was given a sort of hope chest to carry personal belongings, they were girls of marriageable age and said to be of good moral character. The French government encouraged them to go to Louisiana to find husbands, have children and build large, stable families as a means of increasing the population of permanent settlers. The concept proved to be valid: Most or all of the girls were married, and the population began expanding promptly.

CHAPTER 21

Iberville takes over
from LaSalle

In discovering the mouth of the Mississippi and claiming the valley of the great river for the crown of France, LaSalle reached the peak of his career.

After the exhilaration of the discovery, however, it was time for the French to retrace their steps, to gain once more the sanctuary of Canada, where LaSalle was determined to consolidate the vast empire he had won for his king at the expense of so much suffering and hardship.

The expedition began the long journey back up the river, by herculean efforts this time, against the current. Supplies were running low, and LaSalle was in a hurry.

For some days the party subsisted on the flesh of alligators. They arrived at a village of the Quinipissas, determined to seek food. They were feasted by the tribesmen, but attacked in the night. The same thing occurred at the village of the Koroas. The French got out relatively unscathed, but LaSalle was suddenly stricken with a serious illness, probably a fever. He was unable to proceed past Fort Prud'homme, and sent Tonti on ahead of him. It was not until September that LaSalle was well enough to travel the rest of the journey to Canada.

There he found that Governor Frontenac, his long-time supporter, had been recalled. He also found his creditors importunate and, in some cases, nasty.

Determined to shore up his fortunes, LaSalle once more sailed for France. He was not destined to return to the country of his triumphs, however. His return expedition to the Mississippi met with disaster. A faulty navigator put LaSalle and a colony destined for Louisiana ashore on the plains of Texas, then abruptly departed for France.

For some time the colony subsisted, but as supplies dwindled, LaSalle was determined to try to find his way back to Canada and help. On the way, he was murdered by one of his own men, somewhere near the Brazos River in Texas.

LaSalle's dream of an American empire did not die with his death, however, and it was now time for Charles LeMoyne and his pride of young Canadian lions to take the center of the Louisiana stage.

Charles LeMoyne was a native of Dieppe, born in the parish of Saint-Rémy in 1626. As a youth, he joined an uncle in New France, where he won employment at one of the Jesuit posts on Lake Huron. Here he became so proficient at Indian dialects that he was able to take up residence in Montreal as an official interpreter. He was given a grant of land, which he began to cultivate, and soon became a man of prominence in the little frontier town. In 1654 he married Catherine Thierry, a native of the Diocese of Rouen.

The LeMoynes settled in their home and began to rear the remarkable family of sons whose leadership was to gain them the title of the Maccabees of Canada. As his sons grew up, LeMoyne added to their names titles taken from localities near his native Dieppe. Occasionally, when a boy died early in life, his title was transferred to a later arrival. Here is a list of the LeMoyne children with the dates of their birth:

Charles de Longueuil (1656), Jacques de Sainte-Hélène (1659), Pierre d'Iberville (1661), Paul de Maricourt (1663), François de Bienville I (1666), Joseph de Sérigny (1668), François-Marie (1670), an unnamed child (1672), Catherine-Jeanne (1673), Louis de Châteauguay I (1676), Marie-Ann (1678), Jean Baptiste de Bienville II (1680), Gabriel d'Assigny (1681), Antoine de Châteauguay II (1683).

The greatest of Charles' sons, however, and the most important to Louisiana, was Pierre d'Iberville, the third child. At the age of 14 he was appointed a midshipman in the French Navy and was sent to France. After four years' service, he returned to Canada, where he took part in the almost-incessant fighting between the French and the English. Although he fought with only a few hundred men, or small fleets of two or three ships, Iberville possessed a natural aptitude for the tactics and strategy of war.

❪ The Peace of Ryswick left Iberville unemployed, just when the French government sought someone to carry on LaSalle's work in Louisiana. ❫

He began his Canadian career in 1686, when he led a detachment under DeTroyes against the English forts on Hudson's Bay, and aided in the reduction of the forts. Also, with the aid of his brothers, he captured two English ships. He was left in command of the forts and succeeded in 1688 in capturing two more ships.

In 1690 he participated in the campaign against Schenectady and later in the year recaptured Fort Albany on Hudson's Bay, which the English had retaken. In 1694 he captured Fort Nelson, and during the winter of 1696-97 he captured Fort Pemaquid and ravaged the English settlements on the coast of Newfoundland.

In 1697, in command of a frigate, he again entered Hudson's Bay and captured three superior English ships in a desperate engagement. Again he took Fort Nelson, which the English had retaken.

The Peace of Ryswick left him unemployed, just when the French government sought someone to carry on LaSalle's work in Louisiana.

CHAPTER 22

'Re-discovering' the Mississippi

Although the Treaty of Ryswick in 1697 ended hostilities between the French and the English, Jerome Phélypeaux de Pontchartrain, the French minister of marine, still found himself faced with problems.

He knew that the Spaniards were planning to establish a base at Pensacola Bay, and from the limited geographic knowledge of the time, Pontchartrain suspected this was designed to blockade the mouth of the Mississippi.

He also heard reports that the English were planning an overland expedition toward the Mississippi from their seaboard colonies on the Atlantic.

Faced with these threats, Pontchartrain devised an expedition of his own to plant a fort at the Mississippi's mouth.

It so happened, too, that he had just the man to command this venture— his premier Canadian captain, Pierre LeMoyne d'Iberville. Iberville was an experienced navigator and would not make the mistake of missing the mouth of the Mississippi. And if it came to a clash of arms, Iberville had already proved his mettle against the English.

Iberville was given two ships, "Le Marin" and "La Badine," both frigates of 30 guns. Two smaller craft, called *traversiers*, were added to the flotilla, and a contingent of French and Canadians was recruited to man the fort. A company of French marines was also furnished for any skirmishing that might be necessary.

D'Iberville assumed command of "La Badine," with his younger brother, Jean-Baptiste de Bienville, as second in command. "Le Marin" was under the command of the Chevalier de Surgères, while his second officer was the Sieur Sauvole de la Villantray.

The expedition of some 300 men departed Brest on Oct. 24, 1698, and d'Iberville needed only 31 days to reach Cape Français, the northern tip of St. Domingue, the leading French colony in the West Indies.

After a refreshing stay, the fleet sailed on to Léogane, the colonial capital on the western side of the island, for a conference with Jean Ducasse, the governor. There d'Iberville recruited a detachment of "buccaneers" to aid in his colonization efforts. On the last day of 1698 d'Iberville sailed from Léogane, rounded the tip of the island, and set a westward course for the mainland.

After an uneventful voyage, the French fleet reached Pensacola Bay on Jan. 26, 1699. The fleet anchored in the bay and discovered there a Spanish vessel. The next morning d'Iberville sent an officer ashore to reconnoiter. He returned with news that the Spaniards had a colony of 300 men ashore building a fort. The post was called Santa Maria de Galve. The Spanish commander sent word that he would not allow the French vessels to enter the harbor, but they might continue at anchor in the outer bay.

Iberville did not tarry, but set sail westward, convinced that the Mississippi lay beyond Pensacola. He now entered unfamiliar waters, and proceeded with caution, taking frequent soundings and never losing sight of shore.

On the last day of January, the French fleet anchored off Mobile Bay, which Iberville proceeded to explore with a long boat from "La Badine."

The bay extends some 25 miles inland, to the mouths of the combined Tensas and Mobile rivers. At first Iberville thought this might be the mouth of the Mississippi, but nothing in the contours of the coastline resembled what he had been told.

The French landed, built a hut on the shore and explored farther inland. They saw several Indians in canoes, who fled at their approach. Later contact was made with hunting parties of the Bayougoula and Mougoulacha tribes, who shared settlements on the Mississippi. Iberville was careful to maintain friendly relations with the tribes, who could help him with their knowledge of the country.

Once the French were established on the shore, Iberville prepared his two *traversiers* to explore the coastline to the west.

Iberville manned the two craft with his Canadian veterans and the "buccaneers" he had recruited in St. Domingue. The two vessels sailed out of Mobile Bay on Jan. 27 and threaded their way through the maze of small islands that dot this part of the Gulf of Mexico.

> ❝ Suddenly Iberville found himself rising easily on a quiet stream. He had discovered the North Pass of the Mississippi. The water was fresh, and it had a thick, whitish appearance, just as LaSalle had described. On the following day, Shrove Tuesday, he began to ascend the river. ❞

The weather was bad. High winds, torrential rains and thunder and lightning impeded progress and made life in the small boats miserable. On the second day of March, as the two vessels raced along under a quartering wind, Iberville saw to the southeast a line of rocks projecting out from the coast. It was almost dark when he saw a rift in the line of rocks, and he sailed through.

Suddenly he found himself rising easily on a quiet stream. He had discovered the North Pass of the Mississippi. The water was fresh, and it had a thick, whitish appearance, just as LaSalle had described. The rocks he saw proved to be masses of driftwood and mud piled up by the current, blackened with age and cemented together by sediment brought down by the great river.

On the following day, Shrove Tuesday, Iberville began to ascend the river. Two and a half leagues above the entrance, they came to a juncture with two other branches, and a broad sheet of water more than 1,000 yards wide rolled before them.

Proceeding northward, the French passed through a vast region of canes and rushes extending as far as the eye could see. For the next few days they continued up river until March 7, when they made contact with more members of the Bayougoulas Indians.

A tribesman agreed to guide them farther up the river to an Indian village where they might obtain food.

On March 13, the expedition reached the Bayougoulas village on the western shore of the river some 65 leagues from the river mouth. An aged sachem smoked a calumet with Iberville, and the French were given a proper welcome.

Food was brought—an unappetizing mush of sagamite, beans and Indian corn cooked in bear grease—but the hungry Frenchmen made short work of it. Then the tribe staged an Indian dance in honor of the French, and a chief strutted forward wearing a blue coat that had been given to him by Henri de Tonti. Here was evidence that the river was the Mississippi, but Iberville had to be certain. Was there other evidence?

CHAPTER 23

First French colony in Louisiana set up at Biloxi Bay

As Iberville's two *traversiers* continued upstream in the broad, rolling river, the French captain was convinced he had found LaSalle's Mississippi River, but he still hoped for definite evidence of the fact.

After spending the night of March 13 on the river bank, the party rowed northward against the river's current and shortly after midday they were escorted to the main village of the Bayougoulas, a hundred-odd huts surrounded by a 10-foot wall of cane. There were some 250 Indians here, many of whom were suffering from smallpox—added evidence that they had been in contact with Europeans.

On the morning of March 16, the expedition set out northward once more, this time accompanied by Bayougoulas guides. They passed a small stream on the eastern bank (probably Bayou Manchac). Later in the day the French saw on the east bank a high pole, stained with some red substance and adorned with the heads of fish and bears.

Iberville was told the pole marked the boundary between the territories of the Bayougoulas and the Houmas. The Indians called the marker "Istrouma," which the French freely translated as "Baton Rouge."

Two days later they arrived at a landing place where they might pick up the trail to the chief Houma village. Gathered on the shore was a delegation of Indians with a peace pipe. The Houmas were a branch of the Choctaw nation, and the landing place was probably just north of Tunica Island. The village itself lay a league and a half southeast of Clarke's Lake.

After his ceremonial visits with the Houmas, Iberville considered driving still farther north on the river, but decided against it. This must be the Mississippi, and he decided to turn back for the coast, since it would soon be time for him to return to France.

When the party arrived at Bayou Manchac, Iberville decided to explore a short cut to Biloxi Bay mentioned by his Indian guides.

Sauvole and Bienville were ordered downriver with the *traversiers*, while Iberville and four of his men, plus a Mougoulacha guide, set out in two canoes and turned off into Bayou Manchac, through the Amite River, Lake Maurepas, then Lake Pontchartrain, thence into the Gulf of Mexico. On March 30 he camped on the shore some four leagues from where "La Badine" rode at anchor, and lighted a bonfire to attract attention.

By noon the next day Iberville was back aboard his flagship, arriving shortly after Sauvole and Bienville. Iberville was overjoyed to find his brother had, while in the Bayougoulas camp, discovered a letter that Tonti had left on April 20, 1685, when he descended the Mississippi in search of LaSalle's expedition.

In the letter Tonti wrote that he had found the post on which LaSalle had nailed the coat of arms of France at the river's mouth in 1682. There was no longer any doubt that the great river was the Mississippi.

Now was the time to select a site for a French fort to guard the approaches to the river, since supplies were getting low and the ships must soon sail for France.

Iberville decided on Biloxi Bay as the most favorable site, and on April 8 the French began to clear land for their fort.

The work went smoothly and by midsummer of 1699 the fort was completed.

Iberville named it Fort Maurepas, in honor of Count Pontchartrain's son, and then prepared to return to France.

Iberville selected 75 of his best men and six cabin boys to garrison the fort and left them six months' supplies. The Sieur de Sauvole was to be the commander.

On May 9 Iberville weighed anchor and set sail for France in the "Marin," accompanied by "La Badine."

The garrison left behind by Iberville made up the first French colonists in the new colony of Louisiana. The list of names, preserved in the French National Archives, has been reprinted several times, as follows:

❝ *The French saw on the east bank a high pole, stained with some red substance and adorned with the heads of fish and bears. Iberville was told the pole marked the boundary between the territories of the Bayougoulas and the Houmas. The Indians called the marker "Istrouma," which the French freely translated as "Baton Rouge."* ❞

Officers: Sauvole, commandant; Bienville; Le Vasseur de Ruessavel; the Rev. Bordenave, chaplain; Pierre Cave, surgeon-major.

Petty officers: Jean Francois de Vasseur, master of "La Précieuse;" François Guyon, master of "Le Voyageur;" Nicolas la Voye; Pierre Tabatrau, road pilot; Philippe Ley, master gunner.

Sailors: Pierre Hardouin (Ardoin), ship carpenter; Raymond Saintot; Bernard Saurotue; Jacques Roy, ship carpenter.

Canadians: Jacques Bellair, Pierre Pot, Philippe du Coudret, Pierre Tesserontie, Antoine Damedieu, Le Palonaes, Yves Le Roy, Claude Marandau, Jean du Chesne, Estienne Godefroy, Jean Emery, Jean Pintureau, Jean du Boullaye, Jean Baptiste Hervieu, Jean Cabuteau, Vincent Alexandre, Louis Guay, Antoine Olivier.

Freebooters: Pierre Desmarez, Michel Chesse, Nicolas de Sarde, Jean Simonneau, Jean Desplans, Philippe Paget, Pierre Bertrand, Jacques Emerit, André Regnaux, Jacques Carolle, Jean Charnaux, Louis Le Duc, Pierre St. Germain.

Laborers: Jacques Gourdon, edge-tool maker; François Sicaud, carpenter; Estienne Tardif; Henri Croisy; Jean La Porte; François de Salle, shoemaker; Estienne Duguay, baker; Marc Antoine Basset; Claude Berge; Pierre Potuet.

Cabin boys: St. Michel, Pierre Huet, Gabriel Marcel, Jean Joly, Jacques Charon, Pierre le Vasseur.

Soldiers: Daniel Pineau, François Montiron, Jean Desgarennes, Pierre Bosset, Jacques Porche, Heyerome Brouin, Jean Malbecq, Jean Marpeaux, Pierre Godeaux, Guillaume Martin, Antoine Siret, Jean Cheive, Jean du Val, Nicolas la Tuille, Jacques Henry, Pierre Vallet, Pierre Maury, Morgan Nomme, Pierre Cilleaux, Guillaume Tucas.

CHAPTER 24

Getting familiar with the Mississippi Valley

On Jan. 8, 1700, Iberville arrived again at Fort Maurepas, heading a fleet that consisted of the "Renommée," the "Gironde," commanded by the Chevalier de Surgères, and two feluccas for use in navigating the Mississippi.

He found affairs well at the fort, with only four men having died since he had departed. In view of heavy mortality suffered in other early settlements in the New World, this was a remarkably good record.

While Iberville had been absent in France, Sauvole and Bienville had been exploring the country and making contact with the Indians. Sauvole had cemented relations with the tribes living near the fort and had dispatched two of his cabin boys to live with the Bayougoulas and the Houmas, to learn their customs and language.

Bienville led exploring parties to the Pearl River and Mobile Bay and later to the Pascagoula River. He cemented friendly relations with the Colapissas, the Biloxis, the Pascagoulas and the Moctobi.

Since the discovery of the Mississippi by Marquette and Joliet, the great river valley was being visited by more and more missionaries, traders and trappers from Canada, and these wanderers sometimes drifted downriver to the Gulf of Mexico. Sauvole reported to Iberville that two missionaries from the monastery of Quebec had visited the fort. The Rev. François de Montigny had established a mission among the Tensas, and the Rev. Antoine Davion was serving the Tunicas. They visited the fort accompanied by 18 men and stayed for two weeks before setting forth on their missions.

Shortly before Iberville's arrival, however, Sauvole had received ominous news. It was reported that Father de Montigny had been murdered by the Natchez Indians. Sauvole also reported to Iberville that Bienville, on one of his explorations, had met an English ship on the Mississippi, and had persuaded the English to depart. Iberville thus felt that he had to mount an expedition against the Natchez to punish them for the murder, and also to build another fort on the Mississippi itself to prevent more incursions by the English.

A number of men who would become famous in Louisiana accompanied Iberville on his second voyage. Among them were the Rev. Paul du Ru, a Jesuit, as chaplain for the colony; André Joseph Penicaut, a master carpenter who spent two decades in the colony and recorded its early years in his chronicles; Pierre du Gue de Boisbriant, a major in the French Army; and the most celebrated of all, Louis Juchereau de St. Denis, the explorer-adventurer who was to found the city of Natchitoches.

Soon after his arrival, Iberville departed for the Mississippi, accompanied by Bienville and St. Denis. The expedition headed for Lake Pontchartrain, seeking a crossing to the Mississippi and succeeding after a muddy portage near Bayou St. John.

Bienville paddled upstream to seek high ground for a fort, while Iberville returned to Fort Maurepas, where he prepared a *traversier* and two feluccas, plus a force of 80 men to explore the north country and to move against the Natchez Indians.

Since the larger ships could not use the short cut through Lake Pontchartrain, Iberville entered the river through the North Pass. When he arrived at a spot Bienville had selected, 17 leagues from the river's mouth, the combined forces began to construct another fort, named Fort de la Boulaye.

❢ Since the discovery of the Mississippi by Marquette and Joliet, the great river valley was being visited by more and more missionaries, traders and trappers from Canada, and these wanderers sometimes drifted downriver to the Gulf of Mexico. ❣

Louis Juchereau de St. Denis was dispatched by Governor Cadillac in 1714 to establish a post on the Red River. St. Denis chose a site that grew into the present-day city of Natchitoches, Louisiana.

While the fort was being constructed, Iberville sent instructions for Boisbriant and Le Sueur to come to the new fort with another party of men. When they arrived, the combined forces prepared to move north against the Natchez.

Before they left, however, they were pleasantly surprised at the arrival of the illustrious Henri de Tonti, LaSalle's colleague, who came down river with a force of 22 Canadians from the Illinois country.

Tonti informed Iberville that Father de Montigny had not been murdered but was alive and still performing his mission with the Tensas. On hearing this news, Iberville dispatched most of the soldiers back to Fort Maurepas, and persuaded Tonti to accompany him up the river.

The party, now reduced in size, paddled up river, making contact with the Indians, until they reached the village of the Tensas, where Iberville was seized with violent pains in a kneecap, which prevented him from walking. This untimely mishap forced Iberville to return to Fort Maurepas, but he dispatched Bienville to explore the Red River and Le Sueur and de Tonti to ascend the Mississippi to search for copper mines and other minerals reported there.

❢ A number of men who would become famous in Louisiana accompanied Iberville on his second voyage. The most celebrated of all was Louis Juchereau de St. Denis, the explorer-adventurer who was to found the city of Natchitoches. ❢

Iberville was immobilized on the Mississippi for some weeks, and it was not until May 18 that he arrived back at Fort Maurepas. He prepared once more to return to France, leaving Sauvole again in command, and pleased that the colony had been reinforced by the arrival of Tonti. The latter had made several trips down the river after LaSalle's expedition and by 1700 he and his *coureur de bois* were acquainted with much of the Mississippi River Valley and the eastern and northern parts of modern Louisiana.

In May 1700, Iberville sailed again for France. During his absence, the colonists carried out the various explorations he had ordered. Le Sueur led an expedition up the Mississippi to the Sioux country, seeking copper mines, while St. Denis returned to the Red River, spending some six months sloshing through swamps and flood plains. Le Sueur returned with a cargo of blue earth, thought to be copper, which was later sent to France.

Meanwhile, supplies began to grow short. The French had not yet learned to farm in the semi-tropical climate of the Gulf Coast. Fishing and hunting afforded fresh meat, but most of the colonial energy was devoted to the fur trade.

In July, Gov. Sauvole died suddenly, leaving Bienville in command. Supplies failed to arrive either from France or Saint Domingue, and the only food available was baskets of corn traded from the Indians. In addition, disease broke out, and when Iberville arrived again from France in December, he found only 150 of the colonists left alive. It was then decided to shift the fort to a more suitable site. For this new fort, Iberville chose the area of Mobile Bay.

Bienville and his contingent reported from Fort de la Boulaye and helped to construct the new Fort St. Louis de la Mobile on the Mobile River. Larger than Fort Maurepas, which was now abandoned, the new fort measured 325 feet along each of its four walls. When the fort was completed, Iberville felt, it would be a more healthful site for colonial headquarters and would be strong enough to defend the Mississippi Valley from the English, the Spanish or any other intruders.

CHAPTER 25

Louisiana territory taken over by proprietor

In April of 1702, Iberville left his Louisiana colony for the last time, weighing anchor for Cape Français and then for France. Shortly before his arrival in France, Queen Anne's War broke out between England and France. Iberville was given command of a French squadron, and set sail for the West Indies.

He struck a strong blow for France by seizing the British islands of St. Nevis and St. Christopher and captured an enormous treasure on the island of Martinique. He then weighed anchor for Havana to join forces with the Spaniards for an assault upon the British key position on Barbados.

In Havana, however, Iberville fell victim to yellow fever. On July 9, 1706, within two weeks of his forty-fifth birthday, he died on board his flagship.

Bienville, left in charge in Louisiana, sought to deal with the colony's problems. Yellow fever, imported from Saint Domingue, where African slaves had brought it, swept over the colony and carried many to early deaths. Hurricanes blew down houses, destroyed crops and ruined stores.

Bienville pleaded for more help from France, for more suitable colonists and especially for girls of marriage age. In 1704, 23 young women arrived, and they soon found as many husbands. The same ship also brought 75 soldiers, four families of artisans, a curate and two Gray Sisters.

The newcomers boosted the colony's total population to 195, but 94 of these were soldiers and sailors, who could be expected to return to France once their tours of duty had been completed. Another 50 or so were Canadian trappers and traders who roamed far and wide and were seldom seen in any of the settlements. By 1706, the colony had dwindled to 85 inhabitants, but a new influx from France raised the population to 178 in 1710.

In 1706, a census reported that there were 23 families in Louisiana who could be presumed to be permanent settlers and the nucleus around which the garrison and the fur traders revolved. The heads of these families were:

M. de la Salle, the intendent; Guillaume Broutin, Jean Roy, Jean La Loire, Jean LeCamp, François May, Nicolas La Freniere, François Trudeau, Etienne Bruille, Michel Riche, Laurent Clostiny, the Sieur Barran, André Renaud, Gilbert Dardenne, Pierre Broussard, Pierre Allin, Jean Bonobonnoire, Antoine Rinarre, Claude Trepanie, Jean Coulomb, Joseph Penigaud, Jean Sossie and Jean Louis Minuity.

The census also reported there were three widows, Mme. Le Sueur, Mme. Gabrielle Bonnot and Mme. Anne Perro.

Thus, after several years of colonizing effort, the French government had comparatively little to show for its efforts. Deciding that the colony was too much of a drain on the treasury, it was decided to grant Louisiana to a proprietor, after the manner of many of the English colonies.

The man chosen was Antoine Crozat, the Marquis de Chatel, and in 1712 he took control of Louisiana. His responsibility was to supply the colony for its needs and to underwrite all expenses except those of the military. In return, he hoped to reap profits from minerals and trading rights.

The enthusiastic Crozat decided to invest 700,000 livres in Louisiana and quickly sent out the first shipload of supplies. On board, too, was Crozat's new governor, Antoine de la Mothe Cadillac; a new commissary commissioner, Jean Baptiste du Bois du Clos; and 25 prospective brides from Normandy.

Gov. Cadillac found his new post disappointing. He wrote back to his master that "this whole continent is not worth having." Ordered to turn his attention to agriculture, he reported "this wretched country is good for nothing...."

He was, nevertheless, an energetic man, and set about promoting the Indian trade, as well as trade with the Spaniards in Mexico and the Floridas, with the English colonies and with the islands of the Caribbean.

In 1714, he sent out St. Denis once more to establish a post on the Red

C After several years of colonizing effort, the French government had comparatively little to show for its efforts. Deciding that the colony was too much of a drain on the treasury, it was decided to grant Louisiana to a proprietor.)

River, and for this the latter chose a site that was to grow into the present city of Natchitoches. When his post was completed, the romantic St. Denis set out with a pack train and trade goods for Mexico.

At San Juan Bautista, on the Rio Grande, St. Denis was detained by the Spanish commandant, Diego Ramon. While in custody, St. Denis fell in love with the commandant's granddaughter, Manuela Sanchez y Ramon. He was quickly bundled off to Mexico City, where he made a good impression upon the authorities and was ordered released.

He returned to San Juan Bautista and resumed his courtship of Manuela until her reluctant grandfather consented to their marriage. For several years, St. Denis conducted an extensive Indian trade in western Louisiana, and in 1722 was appointed commandant of Fort Saint Jean Baptiste at Natchitoches, where he lived until his death in 1744.

Meanwhile, Cadillac was building other posts—Fort Toulouse at the juncture of the Coosa and Tallapoosa rivers, and Fort Tombecbe on the Tombigbee River—designed to keep the English from infiltrating the lower Mississippi country.

Despite all of his energies, however, Cadillac was something of a misfit in his job. He proved to be quarrelsome and opinionated, and in 1716 he was recalled by Crozat. Bienville once more took over the reins of government, pending the arrival of Crozat's new governor.

CHAPTER 26

The birth
of
New Orleans

By 1717, Antoine Crozat was having second thoughts about his investments in Louisiana. He had dispatched a new governor, Jean Michiele, Seigneur de Lépinay et de la Longueville, to supervise his affairs, and the king had sent out five companies of infantry with the new governor.

The national exchequer was low, however, and the crown decided to increase the taxes on property in France. Since Crozat was one of those who had to dig deeper, he asked to be relieved of his Louisiana responsibilities, since he had already lost some one million livres in that enterprise.

The crown granted him his wish, and sought to find another proprietor. One was at hand. He was that legendary character, John Law, a Scot who had gained an international reputation as a financier.

Many of his ideas on government finance were ahead of his time. He interested the Duc d'Orléans in his schemes, however, and was enabled by the regent's patronage to open a bank in Paris, which became known as the General Bank of France.

Law took up the challenge of the Louisiana colony. He organized the Company of the West to supervise the colony and capitalized it at 100 million livres, half the shares of which were offered to the public. Law received a charter on the same terms as Crozat, and he promised to send 6,000 colonists and 3,000 slaves to Louisiana within 10 years.

The Sieur de Lépinay surrendered the reins of government when Crozat was relieved of his charter, and Bienville once more became the colonial governor.

One of Bienville's first projects was to persuade colonial officials in Paris to provide for the founding of a town and trading post on the Mississippi River, which would improve communications with the Illinois country and Canada and also provide a better anchorage for vessels from France than was available at either Biloxi or Mobile.

Early in 1718, Bienville gathered a work force of 50 men and departed Mobile. Sailing up the river, he chose a spot where the river bends in a big crescent near Lake Pontchartrain.

The site was higher than most other spots along the river, and it was accessible to the sea both via the river mouth and via Lake Pontchartrain. He ordered a site cleared and a town laid out. Work proceeded slowly, and by the end of the year, only a portion of the land had been cleared and a few huts built.

In 1719, a severe hurricane struck, ruining much of the stores and flattening the huts. In 1720, the Paris headquarters sent out Adrien de Pauger as colonial engineer, and he directed the work force in laying out streets and blocks. His plan called for a town eight blocks long facing the river, and extending for five blocks inland.

Drainage ditches and canals were dug. A wharf was constructed. The first church and building to house the municipal authorities were next. Also, a cemetery was laid out. Bienville called the town Nouvelle Orléans, in honor of the Regent of France, the Duc d'Orléans.

In September 1721, a five-day storm destroyed most of the buildings, but the town was quickly rebuilt. The town grew steadily and at the end of 1721 had a population of 147 men, 65 women, 38 children, 28 servants, 73 slaves and 21 Indians.

In 1722, two hurricanes again leveled the settlement, and again it was

One of Bienville's first projects was to persuade colonial officials in Paris to provide for the founding of a town and trading post on the Mississippi River. He chose a spot where the river bends in a big crescent near Lake Pontchartrain.

> *Adrien de Pauger, as colonial engineer, directed the work force in laying out streets and blocks. His plan called for a town eight blocks long facing the river, and extending for five blocks inland. The town, as laid out by Pauger, occupied the site of the present* Vieux Carre *of modern New Orleans.*

rebuilt, this time with several brick buildings. The town, as laid out by Pauger, occupied the site of the present *Vieux Carre* of modern New Orleans.

When Law and his subordinates attempted to find colonists to boost the size of the Louisiana colony, they discovered what other would-be colonizers had come to realize: Frenchmen were not eager to forsake La Belle France. They had no desire to leave what they considered the finest country on the globe to risk the wilds of the New World.

Law and his colleagues, therefore, sought help from the authorities. They were given the right to impress vagabonds, to take men and women from prison, houses of correction and poor farms. They even instigated press gangs to fill their quotas of willing and unwilling colonists.

The impressed colonists proved to be more of a liability than an asset. For many of them, the long voyage in cramped ships, plus the rigors of life in the colony, where malaria and yellow fever were constant threats, proved too much. Scores of them died on the passage out or after they had reached Louisiana.

Others proved to be sturdy and dependable colonists, but most of them, from the busy streets of large cities in France, were unable to cope with the wilderness, a strange climate and deadly new diseases. Soon they became public charges or died.

It became evident that some other means of attracting settlers to Louisiana would have to be developed.

CHAPTER 27

Germans greatly aid colonization effort

Early in their proprietorship of Louisiana, John Law and his associates decided that they must seek farther afield, beyond the borders of France, to find colonists for their settlements in the Mississippi Valley.

Using modern public relations techniques, they spread glowing advertisements of Louisiana throughout the Rhine Valley, particularly in the Palatinate of Germany. Subsequently, thousands of Palatine Germans, attracted by the rich promises of Law and his associates, decided to seek new homes for themselves in Louisiana.

No one knows how many Germans came to the New World. Early estimates set the number from 8,000 to 10,000, but modern research has indicated that this is far too high. Many of the Germans grew tired of waiting in French ports for transportation and returned to Germany. Others took jobs in France. Epidemics killed many others.

Modern research indicates that not more than 900 Germans—if that many—ever really landed in the French colonies.

According to André Penicaut, whose journal is the source of much of the history of the colony during this period, some 4,000 colonists arrived during 1720 in seven ships from France. They were, Penicaut said,

French, Germans and Swiss.

The new colonists were landed at Biloxi and at Mobile, and thus had to make their way overland to their new homes in concessions laid out along the course of the Mississippi.

Many of them suffered hardships during this journey since little or no preparations had been made to furnish them with food and transportation. In 1721 and 1722, other hundreds of German colonists arrived.

Because of oversights there was often not enough food for the new-comers, who were told to subsist upon what they might catch on the beaches. They combed the surf, searching for crabs, oysters and the like, and purchased as much corn from the Indians as they could.

Many starved on the beaches before they could be sent inland to the concessions awaiting them, and epidemic diseases swept away hundreds more.

Those among them who survived disease and starvation eventually settled along the Mississippi River north of New Orleans, a stretch that soon became known as the German Coast.

These settlers proved to be capable farmers and industrious workers, and they provided a valuable addition to Louisiana. In fact, a number of historians have stated that the Germans really saved the colony from stagnation.

No one knows today how many Germans first settled along the river, but a census in 1724 revealed them to be securely established in farms. Here are the family names of those listed in the census:

Anton, d'Arensbourg, Bailiff, Bayer, Bebloquet, Berlinger, Betz, Bock, Callander, Christman, Clausen, Clemens, Cretzmann, Distelweig, Dubs, Edelmeier, Engel, Friedrich, Foltz, Fromberger, Funck, Fuchs, Grabert, Hegli, Heidel, Heil, Hencke, Hemmel, Hofmann, Horn, Huber, Kamper, Katzenberger, Kistenmacher, Klomp, Kobler, Krestmann, Kuhn.

Also, Jansen, Lambert, Lesch, Luech, Magdolff, Manz, Marx, Matern, Merkel, Mayer, Miltenberger, Monthe, Mueller, Muench, Necker, Oberle, Pictot, Poche, Raser, Reinhard, Ritter, Reusch, Richner, Riehl, Rodler, Rommel, Schaf, Schantz, Scheckschneider, Schenck, Schmidt, Schmitz, Strantz, Struempfl.

Also, Tet, Thiel, Traeger, Trischl, Troxler, Vogel, Wagensback, Wagner, Weber, Weiss, Weisskramer, Weller, Wiltz, Wichner, Yens, Zahn, Zahnbrecker, Zehringer, Ziriac, Zweig.

Early travelers boating down the Mississippi have left descriptions of the neat farms and the little white houses standing in great numbers on both banks of the river. They tell how the German farmers rowed down to New Orleans with their crops of vegetables, corn, rice and later indigo, to sell their goods on Sunday in front of the cathedral.

> *Early travelers boating down the Mississippi have left descriptions of the neat farms and the little white houses standing in great numbers on both banks of the river. They also tell how, in the 1760s, the provisions generously offered by the settlers of the German Coast saved the Acadian exiles, who landed in Louisiana as bereft of supplies as had the original Germans.*

They also tell how, in the 1760s, the provisions generously offered by the settlers of the German Coast saved the Acadian exiles, who landed in Louisiana as bereft of supplies as had the original Germans.

The census of 1724 reports the settlers on the German Coast as follows: 53 men, 57 women, 59 children, or a total of 169 persons. Other German settlements brought the total to about 330.

Down through the years, the Germans multiplied as their children grew and founded families of their own. As the Germans intermarried with the French and as they registered their baptisms, marriages and births with French-speaking clergymen, a subtle evolution took place in the original German names. Slowly, they became Gallicized.

Some were translated directly into French. "Zweig," for example, is a German word meaning twig. When the first Zweig registered in Louisiana, the French functionary decided to translate into French, and the family abruptly became LaBranche.

In another curious evolution, Miltenberger became Mil de Bergue, and Edelmeier became Le Maire.

Other German names and the French spelling they now have are Clemens (Clement), Dubs (Toups), Engle (Hingle), Foltz (Folse), Heidel (Haydel), Huber (Oubre, Ouvre, Hoover), Kamper (Cambre), Katzenberger (Casbergue), Klomp (Klump), Jansen (Hentzen, Hensgens), Lesch (Leche, Laiche), Manz (Montz), Mayer (Mayeux), Reinhard (Reynard).

Also, Richner (Rixner), Rommel (Rome), Schaf (Chauffe), Scheckschneider (Schexnayder, Schexnailder, etc.), Traeger (Tregre), Trischl (Triche), Troxler (Trosclair), Wagensback (Waguespack), Weber (Webre), Wichner (Vicknair), Zehringer (Zeringue).

CHAPTER 28

Life goes on in the new colony as Bienville is made governor again

In 1720 the French colony in Louisiana fell upon hard times after John Law's huge economic structure collapsed. Law was hounded out of France, and the affairs of the colony were neglected by the government. Emigration lapsed. Concessions were abandoned. Lack of industry and know-how on the part of many colonists handicapped both themselves and the economic well-being of the colony.

Bienville, operating on meager resources, strove to hold the colony together and to strengthen its foundations. He continued to plead for help from France. In 1722 the first group of *filles à la cassette* arrived. Called "casket girls" because each was given a sort of hope chest to carry personal belongings, they were girls of marriageable age and of good moral character. They were lodged in New Orleans under the care of the Ursuline Sisters, who arrived the same year. All of the girls were soon married.

In 1728 Bienville was recalled to France to give an account of his stewardship, and a new governor was sent out. He was Etienne Boucher de la Perier de Salvert, a former naval officer who soon found himself embroiled in an Indian war. In 1729 the Natchez Indians, coaxed onward by English traders, attacked Fort Rosalie on the site of the present-day Natchez. The French garrison was slaughtered and nearly 300 colonists

> **❝** *In 1722 the first group of* filles à la cassette *arrived. Called "casket girls" because each was given a sort of hope chest to carry personal belongings, they were girls of marriageable age and of good moral character. They were lodged in New Orleans under the care of the Ursuline Sisters.* **❞**

in the area were killed. It was the first serious Indian outbreak in many years.

The French gathered their forces for a counterattack, and in a winter campaign in 1730-31 the Natchez were routed, driven from their forts and harried out of the colony. Several hundred were captured and sold into slavery. The others fled to join the Choctaws, and the Natchez ceased to exist as a separate Indian nation.

The colony continued to make slow progress. By 1728 New Orleans had a population of nearly 1,000 and by then had a handsome brick church on the site of the present Cathedral of St. Louis.

In 1719 the d'Artaguette family had been given a concession of land on the east side of the Mississippi, five leagues above La Manchac. By 1725 land had been cleared and a settlement called Dironbourg had grown up, consisting of some 30 whites and 20 Negro slaves. The settlers, however, persisted in calling the settlement Baton Rouge.

In 1723 a detachment of soldiers was sent up the Red River to establish a post at the rapids. Thus, Poste du Rapides developed into present-day Pineville. New settlements were laid out along the lower Mississippi above and below New Orleans, and along the upper Lafourche. By 1731 the population of the colony was estimated at 7,000.

Governor Perier, like all governors, had his troubles with the government at home, however, and was recalled in 1732. Bienville was called out of retirement, and made governor of the colony for the fourth time.

Bienville arrived back in Louisiana in the spring of 1733, a weather-beaten, yellow-complexioned man of 53. He found the colony growing but the reins of government lax and the military establishment in disarray. Food was scarce and the colony was suffering from extensive hurricane damage.

Before he was able to set many things aright, he was faced with another Indian outburst, this time on the part of the Choctaws and the Alabamas.

Bienville ordered forces upriver and downriver to assemble for a campaign. The upriver force rashly attacked before Bienville and the bulk of the French troops arrived, and was decimated.

Bienville, when he finally arrived, launched three attacks against the strongly entrenched tribe, but each attack was beaten off. He assembled an even larger force later, but in 1740 the Choctaws sued for peace, and a treaty was signed in April.

The last years of Bienville's term as governor were embittered by growing hostility on the part of French officials in Paris. Finally, he gave up in disgust and in 1742, at the age of 62, he asked to be retired. He departed for France in 1743, and disappeared from the colonial stage.

It is no exaggeration to say that without Bienville's patient and untiring efforts, the French colony may not have been founded. His skill as an administrator, his ability to endure hardships, official indifference back home, and the trials that face any pioneer leader, were at times the chief guarantee that the colony would survive.

Bienville spent most of his life in the American wilderness. He was 19 years younger than Iberville, his most famous brother, and was only 19 when Iberville left him as second in command to Sauvole in Louisiana. He became governor for the first time at age 21, when Sauvole died suddenly.

He helped build Fort Maurepas, Fort Rosalie at Natchez, Fort St. Louis at Mobile and posts at Block Island, at Baton Rouge and on the lower Mississippi. He established Mobile in 1711 and New Orleans in 1718.

Bienville surveyed the country, charted its waters and drew the first maps. He explored the Red River as far as Natchitoches, mastered several Indian dialects and waged war against a number of powerful tribes.

Historians have called his patience and tenacity without parallel in the history of European colonization. He built a strong and viable colony in Louisiana despite an indifferent court, jealousy within the colony and depredations by English and Indians.

Bienville introduced the first cattle, hogs and chickens into the colony. He grew and exported the first cotton and tobacco. He experimented with indigo and silk. He exported the first timber and turpentine. He was a sailor, soldier and explorer, but mainly he was a builder, and he had faith,

---

❢ Without Bienville's patient and untiring efforts, the French colony may not have been founded. His skill as an administrator, his ability to endure hardships, official indifference back home, and trials that face any pioneer leader, were at times the chief guarantee that the colony would survive. ❣

---

tenacity, fortitude and frugality at a time when the infant colony needed them most.

One of his last acts was to request the establishment of a college in Louisiana for the education of the colony's youth.

Bienville lived on in retirement in France for nearly 20 years after leaving Louisiana. He made perhaps his last notable appearance in 1762, when he appeared before the officials of the French court in a vain attempt to persuade them not to cede Louisiana to Spain. He died in 1768, at nearly 88 years of age.

Now it is time to retrace our steps to Nova Scotia, to consider the fortunes of the Acadians under English rule.

Part V

The Acadian Exile and Resettlement in Louisiana

Despondent French-Acadians, under guard by British soldiers, wait to board ships and be deported from their homeland in 1755.

CHAPTER 29

Acadians forcibly deported from their homeland

Since 1713, the Acadians had lived under the English flag. The Treaty of Utrect, signed in that year, gave the whole of the Acadian Peninsula to the English. By the terms of this same treaty, the Acadians were given the right to keep their arms, to practice their religion and to retain their possessions. The English often broke treaties, however.

By the treaty terms, for example, those Acadians wishing to leave the province to settle in Canada were to be allowed to go. They were to be given a year in which to prepare to move and were to be allowed to take their possessions with them. Those who elected to remain were assured that they would not be required to bear arms against the French.

Throughout the era of English rule, however, English officials denied permission of any Acadians to leave the province. It was correctly pointed out to the Board of Trade in London that if the Acadians left Nova Scotia, as the English called it, there would be no one left to support the British garrison with food and other supplies.

As early as 1720, members of the Board of Trade considered expelling the Acadians, but they felt their ties in Nova Scotia were still too weak. If the English garrison there needed wheat, or vegetables or meat, they must be procured from the Acadians. The English could not even get the timber they needed to build their forts without the aid of Acadian axemen.

During the War of the Austrian Succession, from 1744 to 1748, the Acadians maintained their neutrality, despite three invasions of Nova Scotia by French troops. Paul Mascarene, the English governor at the time, reported:

"The repeated attempts of the enemy on Nova Scotia have not had the success they expected; and notwithstanding the means they used to entice or force into open rebellion the Acadians, who are all of French extraction and papists, they have been not able to prevail, except upon a few of them."

Despite this fact, the English government turned more and more to the idea of expulsion. A new governor, Sir Edward Cornwallis, was appointed with instructions to take a careful census of the Acadians, to allow no priests to officiate among them and to use all means necessary to have Acadian children instructed in the Protestant religion.

If these measures were not successful, sterner measures would be used. The Acadians sent many petitions to London, asking that their persecutions cease, but to no avail. Now, more and more of the Acadians were leaving their homes secretly and settling in French territory at New Brunswick. Several thousand left Nova Scotia between 1713 and 1755.

For those remaining in Nova Scotia, conditions grew worse in 1753 when Charles Lawrence became governor. Lawrence was a moody, irascible man, known in London for rashness and a quarrelsome nature.

The English citizens of Halifax in 1758 denounced Lawrence as "a lowly, crafty tyrant," and inveighed in official protest against his "wicked mind and perfidious attitude" for "oppression and tyranny." They accused him of embezzling some 30,000 pounds in supplies, and for stealing 1,000 cattle and 3,000 hogs from the exiled Acadians.

As soon as he took over the administration of Nova Scotia, Lawrence moved to expel the Acadians. He feared to drive them into Canada, however, where their numbers would increase French strength.

Lawrence decided to use an oath of allegiance as a pretext. He would demand that the Acadians swear allegiance to the English, even to the point of fighting under the English flag against the French. As he explained his scheme:

"I will propose to them the oath of allegiance. If they refuse, we shall have in that refusal a pretext for the expulsion. If they accept, I will refuse them the oath, saying that Parliament prohibits them from taking it. In both cases, I will deport them."

Preparations were carefully kept secret. Troops were marshalled near the principal Acadian towns. Ships were brought in from as far away as Boston. All Acadians were ordered to surrender all firearms or to be

> **The Acadians were ordered to assemble at their churches to hear an important proclamation by the English government. At all points, the Acadians were told they were to be deported and were immediately held prisoners.**

considered as rebels.

On Aug. 1, 1755, Gov. Lawrence sent out his instructions to his troop detachments: All Acadian lands, tenements, cattle and livestock were to be forfeited with all other effects. All French inhabitants of Nova Scotia were to be removed and they were prohibited from carrying any of their possessions, except as much of their household goods as they might carry in their hands.

The Acadians were ordered to assemble at their churches to hear an important proclamation by the English government. At all points, the Acadians were told they were to be deported and were immediately held prisoners.

In Beaubassin, some 400 Acadians gathered to hear the proclamation. They were all imprisoned, and military detachments were sent through the countryside to bring in all others. Many others, being warned, fled into the forests. Most of them eventually made their way to Canada.

The 400 prisoners, including some140 women and children, were driven aboard ships. There was no room for nearly 100 other wives and children, and they were left behind. Most of them attempted to reach Canada, but the majority died from exposure and starvation on the road.

Altogether, however, some two-thirds of the Beaubassin inhabitants escaped the English.

At Grand Pré 418 men met in the church, and all were taken prisoner. At Pisquid the English took 183 men. At Annapolis, nearly half of the population of 3,000 escaped. Today, the descendants of all of those escaped Acadians total some 230,000.

Those captured were loaded into ships, overcrowded, without provisions and shipped off to strange lands.

Edmund Burke wrote probably the most sober assessment of the expulsion:

"We did, in my opinion, most inhumanely, and upon pretenses that, in the eye of an honest man, are not worth a farthing, root out this poor, innocent, deserving people, whom our utter inability to govern, or to reconcile, gave us no sort of right to extirpate."

CHAPTER 30

Exiles treated badly in British colonies

The Acadians suffered grievously during their days of capture and imprisonment by the English, and even more on their voyages to exile.

In the Beaubassin region, some 400 men assembled to hear the governor's proclamation of exile, and they were immediately placed under armed guard. Military detachments were dispatched to round up all other Acadians in the area.

When ships arrived to take them into exile, the English authorities ordered the men onto the ships first. Some 400 men were taken, and then about 150 of the wives and children. No attempt was made to keep families together, and for the most part, husbands were separated from their wives and children from their parents.

At Grand Pré, some 418 men reported to hear the proclamation, and the same procedures were followed. At Pisquid, some 180 men were taken, and at Annapolis the toll was more than 1,500.

Those who escaped the soldiers had the wilderness to traverse because the English burned all of the houses and farm buildings, burned the crops and slaughtered all of the livestock they did not want for themselves. Those who escaped, therefore, faced the grim prospect of making the long journey to Canada and safety with little more than their hands to sustain them.

On Oct. 27, 1755, 14 ships carrying 1,600 Acadians from Grand Pré and 1,300 from Pisquid and Port Royal joined 10 transports in the Bay of Fundy with 1,900 Acadians from Beaubassin. This was the first wave of imprisonment and transportation that was to continue through 1763, until the Treaty of Paris ended the French and Indian War.

Food and water were inadequate aboard ship. In many instances, the Acadians were crowded into small ships so tightly packed that they could not lie down. The mortality rate was especially high among the old and the young, and this, coupled with no knowledge of other members of their families, made the voyage a nightmare for most.

Husbands and wives, brothers and sisters, parents and children, fiances and friends were separated, they thought for only a few days or weeks, but for the vast majority they were never to meet again on earth. Unknown to them, the ships all had different and far-distant destinations.

Gov. Lawrence had decided to scatter the exiles along the British colonies on the Atlantic seaboard, only he neglected to inform the authorities of these colonies that the Acadians were coming.

As a result, no preparations were made for them. They were dumped ashore with no friends, no money, no food, and only the clothing they wore. Six of the ships, bound for South Carolina, were hit by a storm and forced into Boston for repair. The Boston authorities reported the ships overloaded, with insufficient food and polluted water. They were not seaworthy, it was reported, and the exiles thus were disembarked in Boston.

They were there made indentured slaves. Those who still had their children had them torn away and distributed in Protestant homes in various Massachusetts towns. The Acadians were forbidden to leave the towns in which they were indentured for any reason, even to seek relatives.

Some 300 exiled to New York met the same fate. Colonial authorities complained that Lawrence had sent the exiles "poor, naked, without any of the necessities of life, . . .a heavy burden on this colony."

About 450 were sent to Pennsylvania, where the governor said he did not know what to do with them and demanded that Lawrence take them back. Smallpox soon broke out in the ships, and many died.

Nearly 1,000 Acadians were sent to Maryland, and there alone they received a welcome, since Maryland had been settled by English Catholics, so the Acadians were not considered to be aliens. They were quartered in private homes at first and then helped to find and build houses for themselves.

❢ Gov. Lawrence had decided to scatter the exiles along the British colonies on the Atlantic seaboard, only he neglected to inform the authorities of these colonies that the Acadians were coming. As a result, no preparations were made for them. They were dumped ashore with no friends, no money, no food, and only the clothing they wore. ❣

A suburb of Baltimore became known as French Town, where a church was built for them. Others spread out to other Maryland towns, where many of their descendants still live.

Virginia, too, refused to receive the exiles, kept them from coming ashore, and here, too, epidemics broke out and many hundreds died. Finally, the survivors were taken to England, where they were treated as prisoners of war.

About 1,000 Acadians were landed in South Carolina, where they were indentured to work in the cotton and indigo fields. By dint of much suffering they gained funds enough to buy two old ships and gained permission to leave the colony. Their ships, being unseaworthy, ran aground off Virginia.

There the authorities confiscated all of their belongings and forced them to put to sea again, where they ran aground on the Maryland coast. Finally, they were able to repair the ships, and took to the sea again, finally arriving in Canada after 1763. Of the 2,000 of this group who departed from Acadia, only 900 were alive by the time they reached Canada.

Georgia received 400 exiles, where they, too, were put to work to slave in the fields. In 1758, they received permission to leave, and bought a ship to take them back to Canada, where fewer than 100 finally arrived.

Some 60 percent of the exiles died before they were repatriated, and there were many in every English colony who were never returned because of age, infirmity, illness or other reasons. Particularly melancholy was the fate of hundreds of orphaned children who had been separated from their parents in Nova Scotia, or whose parents died later. There was no place for them to go. Many of them died. Many of those who survived grew up as Englishmen and Englishwomen; their descendants today usually do not know the history of their ancestors, nor that they carry Acadian names. Others were adopted by Acadian families and reared as Acadians.

In Nova Scotia, too, the fugitives who escaped the ships were hunted down by the English and the Indians. The English put bounties on the Acadians and paid for the scalps of Acadians and their Micmac Indian allies.

On May 14, 1756, Lawrence set up a bounty of 30 pounds sterling for each male scalp over 16, and 25 for younger males or women and children. Although this was ostensibly limited to Indians, in practice the English paid the bounties without inquiring into the race of the original owners of the scalps.

The Rev. Hugh Graham, a Protestant minister in Nova Scotia, reported, "A party of Rangers brought in one day 25 scalps, pretending they were Indians, and the commanding officer gave orders that the bounty should be paid." When the man objected, he was told that "the French are all supposed to be out of the country, and. . .there is a necessity of winking at such things."

CHAPTER 31

Displaced Acadians finally settled in Louisiana

The Acadian exiles scattered along the Atlantic coast by their British oppressors naturally made every effort to escape their cruel fate. The British colonists, hostile to everything French, made no effort to restrain them, but also made no effort to help them. The only exception was Maryland, where the Acadians were made welcome, and where many of them settled.

For others, however, their only hope lay in escaping to French territory. They had a choice of four refuges. They could return to Canada, which after the peace treaty of 1763 was in British hands. They could sail to French colonies in the West Indies, such as St. Domingue, Martinique and Guadeloupe. They could go to France. They could go to Louisiana.

All four refuges received their share of the Acadian exiles, but the largest majority finally came to Louisiana. Those exiles in the Southern colonies of the Carolinas and Georgia were, of course, nearest to Louisiana, and they seem to have been among the first to arrive.

Many of them set out for the Mississippi, either by horse and wagon or by riverboat. Some of those in Pennsylvania floated down the Ohio and Mississippi rivers to French territory.

They kept no records, so there is no way of being certain who were the first to arrive, how many they were or from which colony they originated.

It may well be, too, that some of the Acadians who originally fled to Canada were able to make their way to Louisiana by retracing LaSalle's route. But history is silent as to the details.

When they arrived, they probably settled along the shores of the Mississippi, north of the German Coast. Some of them later, perhaps, moved to join other Acadian refugees in the Opelousas and Attakapas areas. It is impossible to ascertain their numbers or to trace their routes, but word-of-mouth tradition has preserved several narratives of overland expeditions making the long and dangerous trip through the wilderness, exposed to hunger and thirst, exposure and Indian hostility.

Acadians who first left the Atlantic Coast colonies for the West Indies also turned their faces to Louisiana when they discovered that the tropical climate and the slave-oriented society of the "Sugar Islands" did not meet their liking.

In 1765, Charles Aubry, the military commandant in Louisiana, reported 60 Acadian families had arrived from St. Domingue, and that there were already so many Acadians in Louisiana that "we do not speak of them in the hundreds anymore, but in the thousands."

When the Treaty of 1763 was signed, many Acadians who had been imprisoned in Nova Scotia were released. Their farms were now occupied by English colonists, however, and they were forced to seek new homesteads and new means of livelihood elsewhere.

Some of them went to St. Pierre and Miquelon, two small islands in the Gulf of St. Lawrence that were still French possessions. Still others went to the West Indies and to Louisiana.

In 1764, a large group of these newly released Acadians, led by Joseph Broussard (dit Beausoleil), migrated to the West Indies. There they changed ships and headed for Louisiana. When they arrived, Louisiana authorities gave them permission to settle in the Attakapas District, in the southwestern part of the colony.

From these original settlers and others who followed them, there descended the present-day inhabitants of St. Martin, Lafayette, Iberia, Vermilion and St. Mary parishes.

The exiled Acadians arrived in the Attakapas country in 1765, and their chief leader, Broussard (dit Beausoleil), signed a contract with a retired French army captain, Antoine Bernard d'Hauterive, who agreed to supply the Acadians with the beginnings of a livestock herd.

In addition to Beausoleil, the contract contained the signatures of Pierre Arcenaud, Alexandre Broussard, Jean-Baptiste Broussard, Victor Broussard, Jean Dugas, Joseph Guillebeau and Olivier Thibadau.

Beausoleil died in October of the same year, probably from the plague that seems to have accompanied the Acadians from St. Domingue.

❨ *In 1764, a large group of these newly released Acadians migrated to the West Indies. They decided to come to Louisiana, and when they arrived, Louisiana authorities gave them permission to settle around the* Poste des Attakapas. *From these original settlers and others who followed them, there descended the present-day inhabitants of St. Martin, Lafayette, Iberia, Vermilion and St. Mary parishes.* ❩

Among other Acadians whose deaths were recorded in the official registers in the St. Martin Parish courthouse are François Arceneaux; Joseph Bellefontaine; Augustin Bergeron; Sylvain Breaux; Alexandre Broussard and his wife, Marguierite Thibodeaux; Victor Broussard and his wife, Isabelle LeBlanc; Jean Dugas and his wife, Marie-Charlotte Gaudin; Joseph Girouard; Jacques Hugon; René Robichaux; and Charles Thibodeaux's widow, Brigitte Breaux.

The registers also announce the christening of Anne Thibodeaux, daughter of Olivier Thibodeaux and Madeleine Broussard. This notice was signed by the Rev. Jean François, who signed himself as *curé de Nouvelle Acadie des Attakapas.*

Throughout the 1760s, Acadians continued to arrive in Louisiana from Canada, Nova Scotia and the West Indies, and joined their confreres who had already settled in the colony.

CHAPTER 32

The Acadians' trans-Atlantic migration of 1785

While a number of the Acadian exiles in the English colonies came to Louisiana, others were finally sent to France. This was particularly true of those in the northern and central colonies. Also, those Acadians held as prisoners of war in England were sent to France upon the signing of the Treaty of 1763.

In August of 1763, for example, 660 Acadians in Connecticut petitioned colonial authorities to be sent to France. There were 249 in New York and 280 in the Carolinas who also asked for French refuge. Another 187 in Georgia and 383 in Pennsylvania were returned to France.

Of some 1,500 Acadians originally sent to Virginia, 866 survived to be returned to France. At the end of the hostilities, the British themselves sent 2,452 Acadians to France. These had been held in England as prisoners of war.

The bulk of the refugee Acadians were settled in French ports in Normandy, Brittany, Aunis and Guyenne, subsisting on the allowance of six cents a day afforded them by the French government. For 20 years the refugees waited, hoping for permanent homes, where they could begin their lives anew. They were doomed to disappointment. There was no arable land available to them in France. The French government, from time to time, attempted to colonize other parts of the French Empire, but these attempts did little to solve the problem.

It remained for Spain to come to the rescue of these Acadians.

In 1762, when they realized that they were losing the war with England, French officials decided to cede the colony of Louisiana to Spain. This would at least keep it out of the hands of the English. It would also reward the Spanish government for the help Spain rendered to France during the war.

Thus, in 1783 the Acadians were still looking for some way out of their dilemma, and the Spanish government was seeking some means of bolstering its new possessions from the forays of the English, who had already seized from France all of that part of North America east of the Mississippi River and north of the Floridas.

The long exile, of course, left many of the Acadians despondent. They were further disgruntled when the French government, in debt from its assistance to the fledgling United States during the American Revolution, discontinued its daily subsidy, and was now furnishing only provisions and clothing.

The Acadians had, for the most part, resisted assimilation into the rest of the French populace, and now found themselves marked out as a separate people. They had become strangers in their own land, and they were not really wanted there.

Into the picture at this time came Peyroux de la Coudrenière, a druggist of Nantes who had spent seven years in Louisiana during the term of Luis de Unzaga y Amezaga as governor.

He become acquainted with some of the Acadians, and in telling them about Louisiana, he seized upon the idea of sending the Acadians to that Spanish colony. He realized that the Acadians already in Louisiana would welcome their kinsmen and would assist them in finding new homes.

He then approached the one man most responsible for rescuing the Acadians: Don Pedro Pablo Abarca de Bolea, Count de Aranda, the Spanish ambassador in Paris. Count de Aranda at once realized the possibilities the idea possessed for strengthening Spain in the colony, and he authorized Peyroux to sound out the Acadians on the idea, after obtaining the permission of the French government.

Peyroux then obtained the assistance of Oliver Terrio, who agreed to see if he could work up enthusiasm among the Acadians for the project. Terrio approached a large number of the exiles, but found only four who were willing to sign a petition to the King of Spain, asking for refuge in Louisiana. Those four were Simon Masrolle, Marin Gatreau, Pierre Jamlo and Etienne Terrier.

Thus, the petition was written and signed and sent to King Charles III of Spain. The petitioners stated that after 20 years of exile, the Acadians were still stranded in Brittany and Normandy, with no lands to farm and no fixed livelihoods.

The arguments of Aranda and Peyroux were cogent: Spain needed colonists to strengthen Louisiana. Heretofore, Spanish authorities had been sending unskilled colonists to Louisiana, people who didn't know how to farm. With well-trained farmers like the Acadians, Spain could dispense with the purchase of slaves, which all agreed corrupted the morals of the colonists and destroyed their purity of language and desire to work. Louisiana was vast and fertile, and Spain should be reaping great wealth from it.

King Charles III was reluctant at first. He felt that the project would cost too much money, and money was hard to come by for governments which had been at war for so many years.

Then there appeared on the scene one of Spain's authentic heroes, the Captain General of Louisiana, Don Bernardo de Gálvez. As his uncle, José de Gálvez, the Spanish minister of the Indies, wrote, the captain general "just happened to arrive for a short time and wished to give the king his opinion in regard to the petition of the Acadians."

Gálvez, who had beaten English armies in the southern colonies during the American Revolution and who had never lost a battle, had a great deal of influence at court.

On October 22, 1783, therefore, King Charles III issued a royal order accepting the plan of Aranda and Peyroux for removing those Acadians to Louisiana who wished to go. He also assumed the expense of transporting and settling them.

In the long history of politics, seldom has money been so wisely spent.

The next step was to gain permission of the French government. Spanish officials wrote to Charles Gravier, Count de Vergennes, asking permission of the French government to settle the Acadians in Louisiana.

On March 31, 1784 Vergennes notified the Marshal de Castries that the King of France had granted permission to the Acadians to leave the kingdom, in deference to the request of the King of Spain.

The summer of 1784 was spent by Terrio and Peyroux in canvassing the Acadians in Brittany to determine who wished to migrate. They found a total of about 2,300 Acadians in France, out of the 8,000 or so that had been repatriated from England. Some of them had gone to French Guiana, others to Sainte-Pierre and Miquelon. Still others had abandoned France altogether. Others had wandered to Santo Domingo, the Leeward Islands, the Falkland Islands, Nicaragua and British Honduras, a few prospering but most living as outcasts and many finally dying of malaria.

Now, there was a renewal of hope. The Acadians assembled in the

> ❝ *On Sunday, May 10, 1785, the frigate, "Le Bon Papa," weighed anchor from Nantes and set sail for the New World. There were 156 Acadians aboard. With fair winds, the ship made the trip in 81 days, a good sailing record, and arrived in New Orleans on July 29, 1785.* ❞

French ports of Boulogne, St. Malo, Rochefort, Morlaix, Lorient, Belle Ile-en-Mer, LeHavre, Cherbourg, LaRochelle and Bordeaux were, at long last, to find a haven.

The entire responsibility for transporting the French Acadians to Louisiana, once the Spanish government decided upon this project, was placed in the hands of the Spanish ambassador in Paris, the Count de Aranda.

José de Gálvez, minister of the Indies, placed unlimited funds at Aranda's disposal. Gálvez made no secret of his eagerness to speed the Acadians on their way "to populate the fertile province of Louisiana."

Aranda found his most reliable ally in Manuel d'Asprès, Spanish consul general in St. Malo. D'Asprès was given the task of drawing up the contracts to transport the Acadians. He also canvassed an additional group of volunteers, and finally was given the job of supervising the removal of all of the Louisiana-bound Acadians.

Meanwhile, Peyroux was gathering data on the cost of the removal. This was a long and laborious process. He gathered bids from ship captains to turn over to d'Asprès. He had to figure the cost of a daily menu of bread, biscuits, cheese, codfish, salt meats and light vinegar. He also had to include such incidentals as hammocks during the voyages, water bottles, bedding, small baskets, measures, lamps and iron-hooped barrels to carry water.

Since the sailing time for a vessel from France to the port of New Orleans might be as much as three months, food had to be stocked for that length of time. There was also the matter of supplying nine lumps of coal per 100 people for heating. In the end, the trans-Atlantic fare for one Acadian came to about $36.

All of these negotiations took months, because proposals had to go from d'Asprès in St. Malo to Aranda in Paris, thence to the royal court in Madrid, and the answers had to be sent back. Thus, time passed, winter followed fall, and it was thought necessary to postpone things until spring.

Finally, d'Asprès signed contracts for seven ships to transport the

Acadians to Louisiana. He notified Madrid on April 4, 1785, that he had completed registering all Acadians volunteering for Louisiana. He had paid each one three cents a day, beginning Jan. 1, 1785, and all preparations had been completed.

On Sunday, May 10, 1785, the frigate, "Le Bon Papa," weighed anchor from Nantes and set sail for the New World. "Le Bon Papa" was a frigate of 250 tons, armed with two cannons, and structured with two decks.

There were 156 Acadians aboard that first ship. There should have been more. D'Asprès had arranged for 39 families to board the ship, but three families failed to report on the day of departure, and the "Le Bon Papa" weighed anchor without them. (Though they missed their first passages, the three families eventually arrived in Louisiana, through the kindness of d'Asprès.)

With fair winds, the ship made the trip in 81 days, a good sailing record, and arrived in New Orleans on July 29, 1785.

The voyage was free from storms, and the passengers suffered no epidemics nor serious illnesses. There was only one death to mar the voyage. The infant daughter of Eustaquis El Joven (Lejeune) died at sea.

Royal orders from Madrid had gone to Esteban Miró, provisional governor of Louisiana, to settle the Acadians with great speed, attending to all their needs as farmers. He was ordered to grant them tillable lands, good homes, farming tools, and a financial subsidy until they were able to support themselves. After 29 years of aimless wandering, such a warm welcome must have overwhelmed the Acadians.

The Count de Aranda had appointed Martin Navarro, intendent of Louisiana, as the official to make proper provision for the settlers. Navarro, in turn, appointed Anselmo Blanchard as his commissioner for the Acadians.

Blanchard began his new duties by going aboard to welcome the new colonists and to begin their registration. And at the same time, the naturalization of the new Spanish citizens began. They were registered according to how the Spaniards spelled their names. French names were

---

❢ *Esteban Miró, provisional governor of Louisiana, was ordered to grant them tillable lands, good homes, farming tools, and a financial subsidy until they were able to support themselves. After 29 years of aimless wandering, such a warm welcome must have overwhelmed the Acadians.* ❢

---

difficult for Spaniards to pronounce, and even more difficult to spell.

Thus, Joseph LeBlanc became José Blanco, Paul became Pablo, Babin became Vaven or Vaben, Lejeune became El Joven, and so on.

Spelling meant little to the Acadians, however, as they gazed on the shores of their new home. They were delighted when Navarro announced that he was granting a subsidy of 10 cents to every family head, seven and a half cents to every adult, and two and a half cents for every child.

With this money, Navarro pointed out to his superiors in Madrid, "they can buy the little things necessary in life, such as wood, tools and so forth."

The expedition remained in New Orleans about a month, in order to allow the new colonists to become accustomed to the climate and food.

Then, with the assistance of Acadians who had long been in Louisiana, Blanchard showed the new colonists their new homes. There were choice farm lands in the vicinity of Manchac, and all but one of the families voted to settled there. The other family, of two members, decided to settle in Lafourche.

Once the choice was made, Navarro ordered that each family be supplied with meat cleavers, axes, hatches, hoes, spades and knives according to their needs. He then had them transported to their new homes on launches and barges.

The first leg of the Acadian expedition had been successfully completed.

A larger number of families were accepted for the second expedition, which was to ship out on the frigate, "La Bergère." This was a ship of 300 tons, constructed in Nantes, and armed with one cannon. With two decks, the ship was owned by Momeron Dupin, and the captain for the voyage was Alexandre Deslandes. The crew was composed of 25 men.

D'Asprès arranged for 73 families (273 people) to sail on the frigate, and before weighing anchor he had the heads of the families elect a board of directors of five leaders to assure that all went well on the voyage. The five elected were Oliver Terrio, who had been of so much assistance to Peyroux in persuading the Acadians to go to Louisiana, Charles Dugas, Charles Aucoin, Simon Dugas and Etienne Dupuy.

On May 12, 1785, "Le Bergère" weighed anchor in the harbor of Paimboeuf and began the long voyage to New Orleans. Once more, the Acadian refugees enjoyed an uneventful voyage, and the ship anchored at New Orleans on August 15, reporting seven births and the death of six elderly people during the voyage.

The 73 families of "La Bergère" remained in the New Orleans area until October 4 so that the refugees could become acclimated, but also because in his haste d'Asprès had sent "La Bergère" off without the trunks and other items of luggage belonging to the families.

When the baggage did not arrive on either the third or fourth ships,

Navarro ordered that the immigrants be equipped with all of the necessary family tools and that they be given lands at once.

Most of the families from "La Bergère" finally settled at Lafourche. The Spanish authorities had divided the colony into 20 districts. Lafourche was, at the time, a district made up of roughly the same area now comprising the civil parishes of Lafourche, Terrebonne, Assumption and that part of Ascension lying west of the Mississippi River.

In 1778 the Spanish authorities had established a military post called Valenzuela on Bayou Lafourche near the present-day city of Donaldsonville. After this, the area was also known as the District of Valenzuela.

Six families of the 73 chose to settle at the Attakapas Post (now St. Martinville), and these families remained in New Orleans several weeks longer. On Nov. 13 they were escorted to their new homes via the Plaquemine Brule River.

One family of three members was settled in Manchac.

On Oct. 8, Navarro reported to his superiors in Spain on the status of the immigrants from "La Bergère:"

"That they might have the greatest liberty in choosing the sites of their future homes, we allowed them to elect their own surveyors.... We did everything to give them good roads that would help them expedite their first harvest."

Meanwhile, back in France, d'Asprès was having no difficulty in organizing the third expedition, which was to be transported on "Le Beaumont," a ship of 180 tons, built in Nantes and owned by Portier & Co. The captain was Olivier Daniel, and the ship carried a crew of 11 men.

The principal leader of this expedition of 54 families was Peyroux de la Coudrenière himself, one of the fathers of the whole idea of sending Acadians to Louisiana.

"Le Beaumont," a newly constructed ship, was fit and fast. Contrary winds delayed her departure for 11 days, but she weighed anchor on June 11 and crossed the Atlantic in 70 days, the swiftest voyage of all the Acadian expeditions.

The ship dropped anchor in New Orleans on August 19, 1785, reporting two deaths during the voyage and some sickness on board.

Once more Spanish authorities equipped the immigrants with all necessary farming equipment, and the surveyors of this group lost little time in finding their new homes.

A total of 41 families decided to settle in the Baton Rouge area. Eight families went to Lafourche and five families decided upon the Attakapas Post.

Before this, however, Navarro had the pleasure of arranging for three marriages involving Acadian girls: François Betancourt to Victoria LaVergne, Joseph Costa to Marguerite Trahan, and Juan Garcia to Francesca Courtin.

By Sept. 9, 1785, Navarro could report to his superiors:

"I gave everyone the necessary tools his trade demanded. I also provided them with a surgeon and medical supplies. Moreover, I placed grinding stones and a big saw at intervals along the road. These tools should facilitate the work of logging trees to build their homes."

Enthusiasm among the Acadians in France continued to grow as they received more glowing reports of the fine treatment their colleagues were enjoying at the hands of Spanish officials.

This led to an unfortunate overcrowding of the third ship to leave France. This was the "St. Remi," the largest ship used by d'Asprès. When the ship weighed anchor and sailed from St. Malo on June 20, she carried 341 immigrants—325 passengers and 16 stowaways.

Smallpox broke out during the voyage, and because of the congestion and overcrowding, it could not be controlled. Twelve children died as a result. Scurvy caused the deaths of three women.

After the "St. Remi" arrived in New Orleans on Sept. 9, smallpox claimed 16 more victims and laid low many more who eventually recovered.

The arrival of so many refugees placed a real strain on the resources of New Orleans. By August the city was overflowing, and Navarro met the challenge by building a huge hall, 200 feet by 26 feet, capable of housing 800 people. He also built two hospitals, one for men and one for women.

As soon as the "St. Remi" voyagers recovered somewhat from their illnesses, Navarro sent out surveyors to find new homes for the newcomers. Lafourche proved to be the choice of 85 families. Two families chose the villages of Attakapas and Opelousas, while two others preferred Nueva Gálvez and Baton Rouge, respectively.

Meanwhile, the fifth expedition departed from LaRochelle on August 12, with 68 families, or a total of 270 passengers, aboard "L'Amitie," or "La Amistad," as the Spaniards called her.

Capt. Joseph Beltremieux brought his ship safely to New Orleans on Nov. 7. By Dec. 15, the voyagers were equipped with farm tools and sent to new homes. The first 46 families were settled at Lafourche. Later, 17 families went to Nueva Gálvez, three families to Attakapas, one couple to Bayou des Ecores, and a lone bachelor was settled in Baton Rouge.

The sixth and seventh expeditions followed swiftly. "La Ville d'Archangel," a large frigate, set sail from St. Malo on Aug. 12 with 53 families, totaling 309 passengers. Sailing slowly, the ship did not reach the mouth of the Mississippi River until Nov. 4, and there went aground. The

> *The Acadians and their descendants have good cause to render thanks to the Spanish government and the Spanish people for providing a happy ending to the Acadian odyssey, after so many years of suffering, anguish and persecution.*

ship had been out of provisions for several days, and had 38 ill passengers.

Food and medical supplies were rushed aboard, and the ship finally reached New Orleans on Dec. 3.

Members of this expedition, when recovered, were sent to new homes as soon as possible—46 families to Bayou des Ecores, six families to Lafourche, while one family remained in New Orleans.

"La Caroline" was the last and smallest ship of the Acadian odyssey. She sailed from Nantes on Oct. 15, and crossed the Atlantic in 64 days. Five days later, she docked at New Orleans with 28 families totaling 80 persons aboard.

By Feb. 8,1786, Navarro had successfully completed the resettlement of these Acadian immigrants in homes of their own choosing. He was pleased to see how quickly they settled into their new homes and began to fend for themselves.

Back in France, French authorities became alarmed at the exodus, and forbade further Acadian departures, lest the area be depopulated. D'Asprès knew that his work was finished, and he was keenly disappointed that he had not been allowed to send several hundred more refugees to Louisiana.

Officially the Count de Aranda reported that 1,596 colonists, representing 375 families (plus 28 stowaways), had been transported to Louisiana at a cost to the Spanish crown of 305,743 *libras tornesas*, or more than $61,000 in the currency of the period. Spain extended an additional $40,000 to aid the Acadians after their arrival in Louisiana.

Thus it was, as Oscar Winzerling wrote in "Acadian Odyssey," that "through the humanity of the Spanish nation, the Acadians at last found a home, arable land, and a new Acadia in Louisiana. There, their descendants today enjoy the right to live in peace and freedom, possess the fruits of their labor, and worship God as did their ancestors in old Acadia."

In service of country, church and state, many descendants of the Acadians have risen to important and exalted positions as governors, legislators, judges, college presidents, bishops and priests.

In fact, Louisiana can point with pride, as Winzerling has written, to the

Acadians of the seven expeditions, who have given, and whose descendants are still giving, so vitally to the political, religious and economic prestige of the American Union.

This colonization effort by the government of Spain was unique in the annals of the North American continent. In fact, it was the largest trans-Atlantic colonization project in the history of North America.

The Acadians and their descendants have good cause to render thanks to the Spanish government and the Spanish people for providing a happy ending to the Acadian odyssey, after so many years of suffering, anguish and persecution.

Spain's part in this trans-Atlantic endeavor proved to be a bright spot in a century marked by wars, bloodshed and political upheaval.

Acadians who made the voyage from France

Following are the names of the heads of families aboard the seven ships that brought the Acadians to Louisiana, along with the number of persons in each family, and the occupation of the head of the household.

Le Bon Papa

Joseph LeBlanc (6 persons), carpenter; André Trample (10 persons), seaman; Joseph Henry (8), carpenter; Charles Landry (9), carpenter; Amable Hebert (6), carpenter; Jean-Charles LeBlanc (2), seaman; Simon LeBlanc (5), ploughman; Alexandre Douaron (8), day laborer; François Hebert (1), carpenter; Anna Boudreau (3), widow; Cecille Bourg (6), widow.

Also Pierre Quintin (5), carpenter; Paul Dominique Boudreau (3), seaman; Jean Baptiste Dugast (4), day laborer; Jean Baptiste Dugast (4), carpenter; Joseph Aucoin (7), seaman; Eustache Lejeune (7), carpenter; Jean Baptiste Lejeune (2), seaman; Gregoire Lejeune (6), seaman; Anselme Landry (2), seaman; Jean Baptiste Boudreau (5), seaman.

Also Angelique Pinel (3), widow; Charles Broussard (7), carpenter; Jean Trahan (1), seaman; Daniel Benoit (3), day laborer; Pierre LeBlanc (6), joiner; Jean Baptiste Guedry (6), carpenter; Louis Stirvin (5), seaman; Elenne Hache (3), unmarried, with two sisters.

Also Charles Daigre (2), block maker; Françoise Boudreau (2), widow; Margueritte LaBeauve (3), widow; Jean Baptiste Legendre (3), carpenter; Jean LeBlanc (3), caulker.

La Bergère

Olivier Terriot (5 persons), shoemaker; Olivier Aucoing (5), carpenter;

Charles Aucoing (2), seaman; Marie Aucoing (3), wife of the absent Michel LeBlanc; Margueritte Noel (2), widow; Simon Mierolle (6), rope maker; Jacques Terriot (3), gardener; Dominique Geruin (3), day laborer; Joseph Guerin (3), day laborer; Françoise Guillot (1), no occupation listed.

Also Margueritte Hebert (3), widow; Antoine Aucoing (3), ploughman; Laure Bourg (5), widow; Charles Hebert (3), ploughman; Claude LeBlanc (3), ploughman; Marie Magdeleine Landry (2), wife of absent Jean Baptiste Commeau; Jean Aucoin (3), ploughman; Marie Anastacie Aucoing (1), wife of absent Joseph Terriot; Pierre Richard (5), ploughman.

Also Tranquille Pitre (4), cooper; Jean Richard (3), ploughman; Marie Jeanne Richard (3), widow; Marin Gotreau (4), carpenter; Chellon Bourg (5), widow; Anne Hebert (7), widow; Ursule Brod (3), widow; Gabriel Moreau (4), day laborer; Pierre Landry (6), colorist; Marie LePrince (3), widow; Pierre Berthrand (9), journeyman.

Also Anne Savary (3), widow; Pierre Gotreau (2), carpenter; Pierre Gotreau (3), ploughman; Jean Baptiste Barillaud (6), day laborer; Widow Hebert (2); Honoré Braud (8), carpenter; Prosper Landry (4), carpenter; Marie Joseph Landry (3), no occupation; Jean Pierre Bourg (3), foreman; Olivier LeBlanc (4), joiner; Louis Letollière (4), joiner.

Also Etienne LeBlanc (1), ploughman; Jean Ozele (6), sawyer; Jacques Douairon (5), seaman; Isaac Hebert (4), printer; Natalie Pitre (3), widow; Cecille Boudreau (3), widow; Amand Pitre (2), ploughman; Amboise Dugast (5), seaman; Olivier Trahan (3), seaman; Marie Brasseur (2), no occupation; Joseph Trahan (5), day laborer.

Also Mathurin Trahan (2), printer; Alexis Daigle (1), engraver; Charles Dugast (6), sawyer; Pierre Dugast (4), carpenter; Anne Ozite Dugast (4), widow; Joseph Bourg (8), sawyer; Pierre Bourg (2), clerk; Jean Baptiste Landry (6), ploughman; Marie Daigre (3), widow; Paul Dugast (3), carpenter; Joseph Dupuy (2), seaman.

Also Prosper Giroir (8), day laborer; Magdeleine Dugast (8), widow; Margueritte Segoliau (1), no occupation; Eustache Daigre (5), carpenter; Etienne Dupuy (2), seaman; Fabien Aucion (2), carpenter; Ambroise Pitre (5), seaman; Joseph Benoit Goutreau (1), ploughman; Marie Rose Livoire (1), no occupation.

Le Beaumont
Simon Daigre (9), carpenter; Olivier Daigre (9), carpenter; Charles Henry (6), carpenter; Pierre Richard (6), carpenter; Pierre Lavergne (4), carpenter; Marie Josephe Granger (5), widow; Anne Granger (6), widow; Joseph Guedry (6), caulker; Charles Commeau (2), carpenter; Jean Baptiste Hebert (3), ploughman; Jean Douaison (3), ploughman.

Also Anne Benoit (2), widow; Marie Martin (5), widow; Pierre Potier (7), carpenter; Jean Douaison (7), carpenter; François Daigle (6), ploughman; François Arbourg (5), caulker; Joseph Trahan (4), no occupation; Pelagie Douaison (3), widow; Jean Baptiste Lagarenne (2), ploughman; Margueritte Josephe Douaison (1), widow.

Also Pierre Hebert (5), day laborer; François Alexandre Daigle (4), ploughman; Moise LeBlanc (5), caulker; Jean Guedry (4), caulker; Joseph LeBlanc (5), caulker; Charles Guedry (5), sawyer; Pierre Guedry (2), carpenter; Joseph Brod (2), seaman; François Xavier Boudreau (2), carpenter; Jacques Moulaison (5), carpenter.

Also Pierre Guedry (7), workman; Paul LeBlanc (5), carpenter; Margueritte Ange Dubois (2), widow; Allain Bourg (5), day laborer; Pierre Forest (1), seaman; Charles Granger (2), seaman; Jean Baptiste Daigre (3), ploughman; Joseph Caillouet (3), carpenter; Jean Pierre Dugast (2), carpenter; Pierre Vincent (1), cooper; Jean Baptiste Duhon (1), ploughman; Jean Charles Richard (1), ploughman; Jean Marie Granger (1), carpenter; Pierre Henry (3), ploughman; Louis François Mont Real (1), domestic of M. Peyroux.

St. Remi

Joseph Ygnace Hebert (6), foreman; Pierre Dugat (4), carpenter; Anne Hebert (4), widow; Jean Baptiste Hebert (6), shoemaker; Alexis Dugat (2), carpenter; Joseph Dugat (11), sawyer; Pierre Olivier Pitre (6), day laborer; Pierre Michel (4), day laborer; Pierre Gautrau (2), carpenter; Marguerite Hebert (4), widow; Joseph Gautrau (8), day laborer; Theodore Bourg (5), carpenter; Jean Baptiste Daigre (1), seaman; Ansleme Pitre (5), day laborer; Anastasie Levron (7), widow; Jean LeJeune (2), seaman.

Also Jean Baptiste Durambourg (3), day laborer; Jean Charles Boudreau (5), wood polisher; Felix Boudrau (2), carpenter; Augustin Trahan (3), carpenter; Gerome Guerin (3), day laborer; Joseph Robichaud (5), day laborer; Marie Hebert (3), widow; Ambroise Naquin (4), ploughman; Pierre Bourg (5), day laborer; Charles Olivier Guillot (5), carpenter; Michel Aucoing (4), joiner; Joseph Hebert (7), seaman; Jean Garnier (4), carpenter; Charles Naquin (7), ploughman; Charles Dugat (4), ploughman.

Also Jean Gregoire Blanchard (5), wood polisher; Hilaire Climent (3), carpenter; Joachin Trahan (7), ploughman; Pierre Trahan (8), ploughman; Blais Thibodau (6), carpenter; Fermin Thibodau (3), seaman; Antoine Boutari (5), carpenter; Guillaume Hamont (2), carpenter; Etienne Daroir (6), tanner; Pierre Theriot (2), wood polisher; Jean Trahan (6), ploughman; Pierre LaBove (3), carpenter; Jean Baptiste Boudrau (4), borer; Honoré Commau (4), carpenter; Joseph Hebert (6), carpenter.

Also Honoré Caret (5), day laborer; Pierre Trahan (3), day laborer; Jean

Baptiste Daigle (4), wood polisher; Atanase Bourgue (5), seaman; Mathurin Commau (1), seaman; Marie Trahan (1), no occupation; Charles LeBlanc (8), day laborer; Joseph Philipe Henry (4), seaman; Jean Thibodau (5), seaman; Ygnace Caret (5), day laborer; Pierre LeCog (6), seaman; Michel Levron (4), carpenter; Eustache Trahan (2), carpenter; Marin Trahan (8), carpenter; Charles Gautrau (8), carpenter; Joseph Richard (2), cooper; Paul Trahan (4), carpenter; Tranquille LePrince (4), carpenter; Charles Richard (2), tailor; Pierre Trahan (1), carpenter; Jean Baptiste Trahan (1), carpenter.

Also Thomas LeBlanc (1), tailor; Joseph LeBlanc (1), employe; Marguerite Trahan (2), widow; Marie Richard (3), no occupation; Alexis Levron (2), carpenter; Lambert Billardin (5), employe; Gregoire Benoit (8), day laborer; Simon Landry (2), seaman; Pierre LeBlanc (6), day laborer; Charles LeBlanc (3), day laborer; Anne Daigle (3), widow; Aimable Landry (4), engraver.

L'Amitié or La Amistad

Jean Gusman (4), day laborer; Jean Broussard (3), carpenter; Charles Doucet (1), carpenter; Jean deLaune (4), carpenter; Jean Baptiste LeBlanc (3), shoemaker; Marie Moise (4), widow; Joseph Aucoin (2), day laborer; Christophe DeLaune (5), carpenter; Jean François de la Marière (5), carpenter; Gregoir Seme (2), rope-maker; Colette Renneau (4), widow; François Landry (4), carpenter; Zacarie Boudreau (4), carpenter; Joseph Boudreau (7), carpenter.

Also Charles Boudreau (3), carpenter; Joseph Semer (3), ploughman; Jean Charles Hache (4), seaman; Ursule Hebert (5), widow; Pelagie Benoit (6), widow; Jean Baptiste Doucet (3), borer; Charles Pinel (4), day laborer; Louis Lamoureux (4), seaman; Marie Joseph Richard (3), widow; Louis Gaudet (5), carpenter; Michel Doucet (5), carpenter; Margueritte Benoit (1), widow; Joseph Doucet (4), ploughman; Widow Boudreau (6); Alexis Brod (5), day laborer; Louis Dentin (8), joiner; Etienne Hebert (7), seaman.

Also Ambroise Hebert (2), joiner; Margueritte Blanchard (2), widow; Benoit Commeau (8), carpenter; Jean Charles Benoit (6), seaman; Etienne Boudreau (9), joiner; Anne Olivier (2), widow; Jean Tibodeau (2), caulker; Ysabelle Boudreau (2), widow; Ursule Brod (2), widow; Eustache Berthrand (6), carpenter; Charles Giroir (2), caulker; Atanase Bourg (4), seaman; Marie Doucet (2), widow; Magdeleine Blanchard (3), widow; Ygnace Amond (4), quarryman; Lusien Bourg (2), carpenter; Jean Bourg (3), rope-maker; Marin Boudreau (4), shoemaker.

Also Joseph Aucoin (1), seaman; Margueritte Boudreau (7), widow; Barille Chaison (5), cooper; Jean Chaisson (4), carpenter; Charles

Blanchard (3), shoemaker; Ambroise Hebert (4), carpenter; François Blanchard (6), ploughman; Françoise Doucet (5), widow; Pierre LeBlanc (3), carpenter; Honoré Duhon (5), carpenter; Chrisostome Trahan (9), ploughman; Jean Metra (German) (3), day laborer; Joseph Benard (Russian) (5), tailor; Bennoit Blanchard (8), seaman; Marie LeBlanc (3), no occupation; Olivier Boudreau (4), ploughman; Marie Joseph Terriot (3), widow; Joseph Brod (4), seaman.

Also Jean Fouguet (4), ploughman; Marie Gotraud (2), no occupation; Marie Henriette Potier (4), widow; Elisabeth Duhon (8), widow; Anastacie LeBrun (7), widow; Ygnace Boudreau (3), carpenter; Jean Paul Trahan (1), seaman; Nicolas Albert (3), carpenter; Pierre Laurenty (German) (3), gunsmith; Pierre Joseph Jacquer (German) (7), joiner; Joseph Pitre (3), carpenter.

La Ville d'Archangel

Marie Richard (2), widow; Joseph Aucoin (8); Pierre Hebert (9); Joseph Aucoin (6); Luce Perpetue Bourg (4), widow; Jean Bourg (10); Jean Bourg (7); Marie Theriot (6); Louis Claustinet (3); Jean Longuepee (11); Alexandre Aucoin (5); Victor Desforets (9); Jacques Desforets (4); Anne Foret (1), widow; Jean Jacques Theriot (6); Ambroise Dupuy (3); Jacques Foret (4); Jean Baptiste Aucoin (3); Victor Boudro (10); Barthelemy Henry (6); Michel Aucoin (12); Claude Aucoin (7); Charles Aucoin (5).

Also Simon Aucoin (6); Marin Bourg (11); Joseph Hebert (4); Claude Guedry (8); Aman Boudro (7); Magdelaine Aucoin (3); Jean Baptiste Aucoin (7); Jean Pitre (8); Joseph Hebert (7); Pierre Henry (3); Jean Henry (6); Ambroise Bourg (11); Charles Henry (5); Pierre Henry (3); Simon Como (10); Ambroise Longuepee (3); Anne Theriot (7), widow; Joseph Ignace Godet (1); Charles Henry (7); Rene Landry (10); Victoire Dugast (3), widow.

Also Anne Joseph Henry (2), widow; Charles Pitre (5); Pierre Arcement (8); Joseph Melanson (2); Charles Thibodeau (7); François Xavier Bourg (11); Jean Baptiste Terriau (3); Le Sieur Pierre Jean Eon, chaplain of Dinan (1).

La Caroline

Jean deLaune (4), ship carpenter; Christophe deLaune (5), ship carpenter; Louis L'Amoureux (4), seaman; Louis Godet (5), carpenter; Michel Doucet (5), carpenter; Joseph Doucet (4), ploughman; Olivier Boudreau (4), ploughman; Ambroise Hebert (4), foreman; Charles Blanchard (3), shoemaker; Basile Chaison (4), cooper; Nicolas Albert (3), carpenter; Ygnace Boudreau (3), carpenter; Martin Pitre (3), carpenter; Claude Louis Legaigneur (2), day laborer.

Also Joseph Terriot (1), seaman; Jean Baptiste Doiron (1), seaman; Joseph Boudreau (2), seaman; Charles Gotreau (4), ploughman; Pierre Montain (6), ploughman; Joseph Duhon (1), ploughman; Claude Marie LeBlanc (1), ploughman; Basile Marie Richard (1), ploughman; Marie Boudreau (1), widow; Jean Charles Benoit (1), seaman; Etienne François Angilbert (foreigner) (3), printer.

Part VI

Epilogue

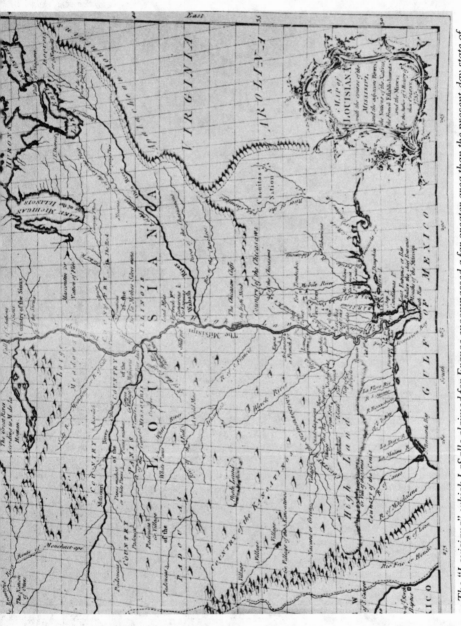

The "Louisiana" which LaSalle claimed for France encompassed a far greater area than the present-day state of Louisiana. As seen in this map – dated 1757 – it included most of the land drained by the Mississippi-Missouri river system.

CHAPTER 33

Trailblazers
of the Western lands

During the era of French and Spanish dominion, "Louisiana" meant much more than the state as it is known today. In Iberville's time, "Louisiana" meant all of the vast territory drained by the Mississippi-Missouri river system—except that area east of the Mississippi already in the hands of European nations.

French influence was strong in Louisiana, and French explorers were among the first white men to reach the territories that made up this vast region. We have seen how Henri di Tonti and his fur trappers and traders began to make regular voyages on the Mississippi and its tributaries shortly after Iberville founded Fort Maurepas.

Other trappers and traders drifted downriver from Canada and spread throughout the region, moving up tributary rivers in their facile canoes. In many instances, they found that French missionaries had preceded them. The French in Canada regularly sent out missionaries—mostly Jesuits— to make further attempts at converting the Indian tribes to Christianity. That this effort was extensive is attested to by the fact that in 1721 the Rev. Pierre de Charlevoix was sent downriver from Canada for an inspection trip to the Jesuit missions.

Thus, during the decades following the founding of the French settlement on the Gulf of Mexico, dozens of missionaries and anonymous *coureurs de bois* found their way west from Canada and southwest through the western reaches of the great river basin.

Early in the history of Canada, this penchant of the French for wandering in the wilds was notable.

Official French policy was to centralize the fur trade at well-established depots, and to encourage the Indian tribes to bring their furs to Montreal or Three Rivers. Enterprising young Frenchmen, however, saw no reason why they should not themselves go to the Indians and trade on the spot. They started out with canoes in the fall or spring, and would not return for 18 months or longer, sometimes spending one or two winters with the tribes in the wilds.

French authorities sought to halt this illegal trade, but had little success. These nomadic Frenchmen were a new breed, distinct from the town-dweller and the farmer. They had an instinct for adventure and a knack for adapting themselves to any sort of environment. Many of them became remarkable backwoodsmen, and in some respects excelled over the Indians as hunters and trappers.

The prototype of these *coureurs de bois* was Etienne Brule, who came to the New World with Champlain, as was noted in an earlier chapter. No doubt Champlain set him to learning the various Indian dialects, so that he might become an interpreter. Brule found the wilds to his liking, for he soon deserted the settlements and spent most of his remaining years in the forest. He wandered far and wide, wrote no books and drew no maps—and seemed to have no serious purpose in his wanderings. Evidently he liked to be on the move, with a paddle in his hand and his eye on the far horizon.

He was probably the first of the Europeans to master the Algonquin and the Huron dialects. Canadian historians credit him with being the first white man to make the long journey from Quebec to Lake Huron by way of the Ottawa River, the first to enter what is now the Province of Ontario, the first to sail on Lake Ontario, the first to visit the Niagara Peninsula, the first to cross northern New York and to descend the Susquehanna River, passing on his way through parts of Pennsylvania and Maryland, and touching the soil of Virginia. He was also the first to stand on the shores of Lake Superior.

His contemporaries did not speak well of Brule. He was unpopular with the Jesuits because he "went native." It is said that he came to an unfortunate end: The Hurons killed him, and then ate him.

Brule was not alone in seeking the solitary life beyond the horizons. He was merely the first of many. Nor was the temptation of the wilds felt only by the French; it was a problem for all harried officials seeking to plant well-ordered European colonies on New World soil.

The westward impulse was strong in Louisiana, too, after Iberville had planted a French colony at Biloxi. The Mississippi now became the avenue of commerce and discovery, and three of its great tributaries, the Red, the Arkansas and the Missouri rivers, became the logical highways for penetrating the Great Plains in search of fur-bearing animals and the traders' promised land of New Mexico.

Given the broad avenue of the St. Lawrence River, which knifed deep into the continent, almost to the Great Lakes, it was understandable that the French would reach the interior before other colonists who found the way west barred by the Appalachian highlands.

And far westward the French travelled. Because so many of them were, in the eyes of French officials, engaged in an illegal activity, few of them boasted about it. They kept no journals, made no reports, and erected no monuments.

They left their mark on the land, however, and we catch tantalizing glimpses of their activities in the journals of missionaries and accounts of later explorers. There was a legend current among the Sioux in historical times that the French had ascended the Missouri River as far as the villages of the Aricara by the 1630s. The "long-beards" sought the skin of the beaver, old men of the Sioux recounted to later historians.

French penetration of the West was first launched from the St. Lawrence River Valley, but after Marquette and LaSalle explored the Mississippi River, and after the founding of Iberville's colony at Biloxi, the center of Western exploration and exploitation gradually shifted to the colony of Louisiana. The Mississippi and its tributaries became the highways to "the Great West."

This penetration was stimulated by three major impulses. First, besides the adventuresome urge to see what was over the next hill or around the next bend of the river, was the search for the beaver. The fur trade lured the *coureurs de bois* farther and farther into the wilds as the supply of beavers became exhausted in one locality after another.

A second lure was the fabled Straits of Anian, which supposedly led to the Orient, where vast riches awaited the ambitious entrepreneur. Third, there were the Spanish colonies—New Mexico, in particular—said to be rich in gold, silver and copper—and ready to trade these and other goods for commodities the French could offer.

After Marquette and LaSalle, the thrust westward was led by the fur traders. Daniel Greysolon, Sieur du L'Hut, traveled overland between Lake Superior and the Mississippi River between1678 and 1681. He made the first historical contact with the Sioux, who told him of a great salt sea to the west (Great Salt Lake?).

Jacques de Noyon made contact with the Assiniboines at Rainy Lake, and he accompanied them as far as the Lake of the Woods about 1687. Rebutel de la Noue and Joseph LaFrance pushed farther into the interior.

But the ablest explorer of the Northern Plains was Pierre Gaultier de La Verendrye. A fur trader on Lake Superior in 1726, he offered to lead an expedition to find the fabled Western Sea. In a series of thrusts into the interior, Verendrye and his sons reached the Missouri River by an overland route, ascended that river to the Mandan villages, and went beyond into the Bad Lands of the Dakotas, eventually reaching the foothills of the Rockies in Shoshone country. Had the French government given Verendrye and his sons even the most modest support, as much as half of that later accorded Lewis and Clark, he might well have forced his way to the Pacific Ocean in spite of all the odds.

By the 1740s, therefore, the French from the Great Lakes had ascended the Kaministikwia River and discovered Rainy Lake and Lake of the Woods, discovered the Grand Portage route, followed the Roseau to the Red River, and ascended the Winnipeg River to Lake Winnipeg. They explored the Red River to the mouth of the Assiniboine River, and crossed the plains to the Missouri. They explored the Missouri westward nearly to the Rockies. From Lake Winnipeg they discovered Lakes Manitoba, Winnipegosis and Dauphin. They had descended the Saskatchewan River and followed one of its tributaries far out on the plains.

The westward impulse was strong in Louisiana, too, after Iberville had planted a French colony at Biloxi. The Mississippi now became the avenue of commerce and discovery, and three of its great tributaries, the Red, the Arkansas and the Missouri rivers, became the logical highways for penetrating the Great Plains in search of fur-bearing animals and the traders' promised land of New Mexico.

Iberville hoped to profit from the *coureurs de bois* by giving them freedom of trade and encouraging their forays into the western marches. In his report of 1700, Iberville mentioned that there were many *coureurs de bois* with the Sioux and other distant tribes who would be willing to sell furs to French merchants. Henri di Tonti, LaSalle's lieutenant, became the commander of a brigade of fur trappers and traders who paddled up the three great tributaries during the decades that followed LaSalle's death.

160

As the French ventured farther westward, however, they became cognizant of two major obstacles. One was the Indian tribes who populated the banks of the great rivers. These tribes were not themselves particularly hostile to the French, but they were reluctant to permit the French to travel farther inland, for there were other tribes, mortal enemies. At all costs they wished to prevent the French from supplying these inland tribes with guns.

The Spaniards, too, were loath to have the French too near. In the power politics of the day, the Spaniards saw the French as rivals seeking to wrest the Texas and New Mexico colonies from Spanish grasp.

Iberville decided early that further explorations of the Mississippi were necessary. Pierre LeSueur, who had traded on the upper Mississippi for some years prior to 1695, was sent north again to explore for mineral riches. In 1700 he ascended the Minnesota River to the mouth of the Blue Earth River near present-day Mankato, where he built Fort L'Huillier. He failed to find the kind of mineral riches that Iberville had hoped for, however.

In 1713, Governor Cadillac called upon a young uncle of Iberville's wife, Louis Antoine Juchereau de Saint-Denis, to lead an expedition up the Red River, and to select a site for a fort as a barrier to Spanish expansion from Texas.

Saint-Denis, who had come to Louisiana in 1699 with Iberville, had been trading along the Red and Mississippi rivers, and was to become one of the more romantic figures in Louisiana history.

Saint-Denis departed up the Red River in 1714 and selected a post which would become the city of Natchitoches. Once the post was set up and occupied, he took it upon himself to seek open trade with the Spaniards. He set off with a pack train and trade goods to San Juan Bautista, on the Rio Grande, where the Spanish commandant took him prisoner. Saint-Denis was sent to Mexico City, where he charmed and disarmed the Spanish authorities, who released him, and sent him to San Juan Bautista again. There he wooed and won the granddaughter of the commandant, and returned to Natchitoches, where he was commandant until his death in 1744.

Past Natchitoches the Red River takes a northerly bearing. The French thought this might be a route to New Mexico via which they could avoid the Spanish authorities in Texas. So, Bernard La Harpe was sent out by Bienville in 1718 to find out if a suitable route could be established.

La Harpe traveled up the Red River for a considerable distance into Oklahoma, probably as far as the western edge of the Ouachita Mountains, and then crossed overland northward to the Canadian River, followed it to the Arkansas River, and descended it to the Arkansas Post.

161

> *In 1739, a group of French traders headed by Paul and Pierre Mallet actually reached Santa Fe and opened the Santa Fe trade.*

One of La Harpe's objectives was to make contact with the Pawnee and the Comanche tribes, of whom the French had been hearing for several years, believing that these two tribes traded with the Spaniards in New Mexico. La Harpe failed in this objective, but he met and opened trade relations with a number of previously unknown tribes before returning to Bienville's headquarters.

La Harpe, too, brought back descriptions of the plains—the vast reaches, the river bottoms thickly covered with trees and brush, and always the incessant wind which blew forever over the moving grasses. He also described the Red River as a new kind of river to the French—streams choked with sandbars, where snags lurked, frequently blocked with matted "rafts" of tree trunks, their channels shifting and treacherous, now deep and now shallow, and everywhere subject to tremendous floods.

The focus now switched to the Missouri River. Perhaps it would provide a path to the Pawnees and the Comanches, and thence to trade with New Mexico. In 1719, Bienville sent Charles Claude du Tisne to find out. Du Tisne had come to Louisiana with Bienville. In 1719 he set out from Kaskaskia and traveled up the Missouri to the Osage River, and then to the Osage villages. He obtained horses from the Osages, and from there penetrated to the Panis villages in Oklahoma, trading with them, too. He found, however, that the Panis would not allow him to go farther to meet with their enemies, the Comanches.

Du Tisne made a swift detour around their villages, however, and went on toward the Southwest until he met a wandering band of Pawnees on the Arkansas River in the middle of modern Kansas. The Pawnees had Spanish trade goods, but could not—or would not—tell du Tisne much about the geography between the Arkansas River and New Mexico. Du Tisne had to be content with what he had learned, and he returned to Kaskaskia.

In 1723 another provocative figure arrived on the Louisiana scene. In order to forestall what he feared might develop into an attack by the Spaniards upon the Illinois country, Bienville sent out a force to erect a fort on the Missouri. In charge of this expedition was Etienne de Bourgmond, one of the most fascinating figures in the Louisiana frontier history.

162

Bourgmond started his career in New France as a government official in Quebec and Detroit. He became a commandant at the latter post, succeeding di Tonti. About 1706, at the latter post, he became enamored of a married lady and deserted his post, fleeing with his new love into the wilds around Lake Erie, where the pair, with other French deserters, lived like the Indians.

With the onset of winter, however, Bourgmond gave himself up to Governor Frontenac, who pardoned him and ordered the errant lady to return to her husband. In 1712 Bourgmond again succumbed to feminine wiles, this time those of an Indian lass. Again he deserted and travelled with his dusky companion up the Missouri River several hundred leagues to her native village. In 1714 he travelled farther up the Missouri as far as the villages of the Aricaras and the Caricaras, then up the Platte across Nebraska and perhaps into eastern Wyoming.

In 1718 Bourgmond was back in Louisiana, this time in New Orleans, where he made the acquaintance of Bienville. When the latter decided to establish a fort on the Missouri, he recalled Bourgmond, who was then living in Paris. Bourgmond left New Orleans in February of 1723. In November of that year he built Fort Orleans on the north branch of the Missouri in what is now Carroll County, Missouri.

It remained for "private enterprise" to accomplish what earlier expeditions had started. In 1739, 15 years after Bourgmond's travels, a group of French traders headed by Paul and Pierre Mallet actually reached Santa Fe and opened the Santa Fe trade.

The Mallets and six companions decided to open up trade with the Spanish settlements in New Mexico on their own. They set out up the Missouri River. They advanced into northern Nebraska, some 275 miles above the mouth of the Platte, to the mouth of the Niobrara. Thence, probably acting on advice from the Pawnees, they struck out in a southwesterly direction.

They crossed the Platte again and the Republican, and reached the valley of the Arkansas in western Kansas. They followed the river farther upstream, and were fortunate to find a friendly Indian who offered to guide them to the Raton Mountains and to Taos.

They surprised the Spaniards by coming into Santa Fe, and while their presence there was illegal, the Spanish authorities chose to do nothing about it. The Mallets wintered in Santa Fe and then returned to Louisiana via the Pecos Corridor, the Canadian River and the Arkansas.

In 1741 Bienville sent Fabry de la Bruyere and four members of the Mallet party back to Santa Fe to propose further trade relations with the governor of New Mexico. This party reached the Canadian River, but low water and hostile Indians delayed them, and finally they turned back.

The situation remained in limbo until 1763, when France secretly deeded Louisiana to Spain. That brought to the fore one of the most effective explorers of the South Plains. He was Pierre Vial, a native of Lyons, who came to Louisiana and traded on the Missouri before the American Revolution.

In 1786 the Spanish authorities sent him on an expedition to open a trail from San Antonio to Santa Fe. Travelling with only one companion, Vial followed the Red River to the villages of the Comanches, and thence overland to Santa Fe. In 1787 he travelled eastward along the Texas panhandle and down the Red River to Natchitoches to establish the first overland route from Santa Fe to New Orleans.

In 1792-93, Vial made the first transit of what was to become the Santa Fe Trail, from Santa Fe to St. Louis (2,279 miles). In 1797 Vial spent two years among the Comanches, and in 1799 he was living near St. Louis. In 1803 he was back in Santa Fe, and in 1805 was trading along the Missouri again.

Vial wrote his reports in rather poor French. Evidently he wrote no Spanish. He seems to have been conversant in many Indian dialects. He died in Santa Fe in 1814 after an unprecedented career as a trailblazer. For 30 years he roamed the wilderness, seemingly at will, safely travelling among Apaches, Utes, Kiowas, Comanches, Kansas, Osages, Otoes, Missouris, Iowas, Sioux, Arapahoes and Pawnees.

Vial and the others mentioned were the "official" explorers and trailblazers. Yet behind the lines in history books from time to time we catch glimpses of other, shadowy figures who were already there when the "official explorers" arrived. There is little data on them, usually no more than their names.

When Le Sueuer, for example, made his long voyage from Biloxi and the Mississippi up into Minnesota in 1700 he reported he found four French trappers on the Wisconsin River who had been trading in Sioux country. When he built his post on the Blue Earth River, near present-day Mankato, and wintered there, he reported that seven more French trappers

---

❦ *Even after the Louisiana Purchase, the French remained prominent in the exploration of the West and the development of the fur trade in the Rocky Mountains. French "mountain men" broke the trails and set the stage for the heyday of the fur trade during the first half of the 19th century.* ❦

> *Throughout the vast region that LaSalle had claimed for France, French trappers and traders, along with Franciscan, Dominican and Jesuit missionaries, formed the spearhead of civilization.*

wandered in from the western country.

In 1705 an adventurer known only as Laurain arrived at Biloxi and gave Bienville a confused tale of travel up the Missouri to New Mexico. A year later, another adventurer, named Derbanne or Darbonne, said he travelled up the Missouri for 1,000 miles to Spanish towns.

The Lewis and Clark expedition journal provides additional glimpses at some of the French traders in the western country. Toussant Charbonneau, who was hired as an interpreter, is one of them. He had lived among the Hidatsas for years. After the expedition built a winter camp at the confluence of the Knife and Missouri rivers, and after making the rounds of the Mandan villages, Lewis and Clark hired another interpreter, Rene Jusseaume, who had lived among the Knife River tribes for years. They also reported on a Peter Cruzatte, who spent two winters among the Indians at the mouth of the Platte.

Between St. Charles and the Kansas River, the expedition met eight rafts or canoes with traders from the Osage and the Kansas tribes. They also met Pierre Doiron, who had lived for 20 years on the Des Moines and James rivers with the Yankton Sioux.

In the vicinity of present-day Pierre, South Dakota, the expedition encountered three French traders, one of whom could speak English. He had spent the previous winter 300 leagues up the Cheyenne River. He told Lewis and Clark of encountering a huge bear, a white-booted turkey and a quadruped with large, circular horns. Thus they learned for the first time of the grizzly bear, the sage grouse and the bighorn sheep. At this time, the expedition was 1,400 miles up the Missouri River.

We also read of Francois Antione Laroque, who seems to have been the first white man to visit the Yellowstone. Pierre Truteau wrote that a French trader named Pierre Menard had spent several years among the Crows and the Gros Ventre.

These are a few of the Frenchmen who pushed into the wilderness ahead of civilization. How many hundreds of others were there whose names have been forgotten and whose trails have dimmed? How many hundreds of other Frenchmen formed the backbone of expeditions led by others?

When Alexander Mackenzie, for example, pushed from Fort

Chipeweyan in 1789 and reached the Arctic Ocean, his party included four Frenchmen, only two of whom—Joseph Landry and Charles Doucette—were named. In 1793, when he crossed the Rockies to the Pacific, Mackenzie was accompanied by Landry, Doucette and four other Frenchmen, unnamed.

Even after the Louisiana Purchase, the French remained prominent in the exploration of the West and the development of the fur trade in the Rocky Mountains. French "mountain men" broke the trails and set the stage for the heyday of the fur trade during the first half of the 19th Century.

Men of French blood, to a great extent, are the ones who manned this first industrial enterprise in the Rocky Mountain West. They carried on the necessary work of the trade—manning the keel boats, seeking out and trading at Indian villages, trapping the beaver, hunting meat animals, and all the other chores.

During the years between 1800 and 1840 this trade was expanded into and across the Rockies to the Pacific Ocean. By the time the fur trade went into its final decline, every mountain peak, every stream, valley and natural landmark between the Missouri River and the Pacific had been discovered.

There were literally thousands of men of French ancestry in the fur trade—far more than men of Anglo-Saxon heritage. One example that might be cited is the Robidoux family. There were five brothers: Antoine, Francois, Joseph, Louis and Michel. They explored nearly the entire West by themselves.

Antoine is fabled as the first fur trader based in Taos, New Mexico, operating there in the early 1820s. In 1828 he moved on to build a trading post on the Gunnison River in the wilderness of Colorado. Four years later, he established Fort Robidoux, or Uinta, in equally wild Utah.

After his fur-trading days, Joseph became a town builder and laid out expansion plans for the City of St. Louis, Missouri, in 1843. Louis developed the Jurupa Rancho in California, which became the nucleus of

---

❨ *French trading posts were established on sites which were to become St. Joseph, Lafayette, Fort Wayne and Fort Clarke in Indiana; Kaskaskia, Cahokia and Fort Charles in Illinois; and Omaha in Nebraska. Jean Baptiste Point du Sable established a trading post in the 1770s on the spot that was to become Chicago.* ❩

> *All of these were French, and they left their marks if not their names upon all of the vast territories west of the Mississippi. Their work, too, is a part of Louisiana's French heritage.*

the city of Riverside. Mount Robidoux is named for him.

Antoine Leroux was another French trader whose activities as a trailblazer and guide were important. He wandered all over the West and knew most of its major geographic features. He was a guide for Col. Philip St. George Cook in the Mexican War, and led Capt. Lorenzo Sitgreaves' expedition from Zuni to San Diego in 1851. He guided John Russell Bartlett on the Mexican boundary survey in 1852, and was with Capt. John W. Gunnison in 1853 on a railroad survey.

Etienne Provost was John James Audubon's guide on the Upper Missouri, and he may well have been the first white man to see the Great Salt Lake and the South Pass.

When Gen. John C. Fremont, the "Pathfinder," set out on his explorations, he was canny enough to engage three French guides to find the paths that he wanted to find. The Lajeunesse brothers—Basil, Charles and Francois—were prominent in Fremont's travels. Basil led Fremont's first and third expeditions, and lost his life on the third, in 1846. Francois was on the second expedition. Charles also operated trading posts in Wyoming. His nickname was "Simoneaux," and the Seminoe Mountains of Wyoming may have been named in his memory.

Not to be overlooked among the early mountain men was Jacques de la Ramee, who wandered through the Mountain West for years, and whose name, though misspelled, has been given to a city, town, river, fort, plain, mountain range, mountain peak and county in Wyoming. He met his death at the hands of Indians on the bank of the stream named for him, the Laramie River.

Throughout the vast region that LaSalle had claimed for France, French trappers and traders, along with Franciscan, Dominican and Jesuit missionaries, formed the spearhead of civilization.

Pierre Laclede went north from New Orleans to found St. Louis, Missouri, in 1764. French trading posts were established on sites which were to become St. Joseph, Lafayette, Fort Wayne and Fort Clarke in Indiana; Kaskaskia, Cahokia and Fort Charles in Illinois; and Omaha in Nebraska.

Jean Baptiste Point du Sable established a trading post in the 1770s on the spot that was to become Chicago.

These examples could be multiplied a dozen-fold. As long as the frontier was there, the French *coureurs de bois* and *voyageurs* were in the vanguard. And when the frontier disappeared, they disappeared with it. Those who survived went back to places like St. Joseph and St. Louis and lived out their lives in the memories of their youth.

These adventurers were followed by the missionaries and the traders, and they, in turn, gave way to permanent settlers. All of these were French, and they left their marks if not their names upon all of the vast territories west of the Mississippi. Their work, too, is a part of Louisiana's French heritage, and although the very identities of many of them have been lost to history, their handiwork has survived them in the broad acres and the busy cities of a dozen or more American states.

–The End–

About the author...

TRUMAN STACEY, editor of the *Lake Charles (Louisiana) American Press* from 1961 through 1981, completed his 50th year as a journalist in 1990.

He joined the *American Press* as a sports editor after having worked as a reporter for the *Beaumont (Texas) Enterprise*, the Oklahoma City *Daily Oklahoman*, the *Detroit Free Press* and the *Washington (D.C.) Times Herald*. Previous to that he earned bachelor's and master's degrees in history and political science from the University of Detroit.

Stacey was the organizer and first president of the Southwest Louisiana Chapter of the Council for the Development of French in Louisiana (CODOFIL) and is currently serving as a member of the CODOFIL State Board of Directors.

After retiring as editor of the *American Press*, Stacey was called back into service as director of communications for the Catholic Diocese of Lake Charles, a position he held through September of 1990.

Stacey has been decorated by two Popes for his service to the Catholic Church. He is a Knight Commander of the Order of St. Gregory the Great, a Knight Commander With Star in the Order of the Holy Sepulchre, and a Chevalier of the French National Order of Merit. He's held a number of state and national offices with the Knights of Columbus, the National Catholic Committee on Scouting and the Boy Scouts of America.

A native of Texas, he has lived in Lake Charles since 1950.

JAMES DOMENGEAUX

Congressman, lawyer and leader of a cultural revolution

As a congressman, he supported good government in his home state. As a lawyer, he defended the rights of the poor and the powerless. As the founder of the Louisiana French renaissance movement, he led the struggle to preserve the language, culture and dignity of the Cajun people.

By PHILIP F. DUR

James Domengeaux was the founder and for 20 years the chairman of the Council for the Development of French in Louisiana (CODOFIL), a state agency dedicated to the preservation of the French language and culture in the state he called home.

An Acadian by birth, he was also a highly successful attorney whose credits include defense of the poor and powerless and whose law firm pioneered in certain kinds of maritime law dealing with offshore oil rigs.

(Continued)

(This article on Mr. Domengeaux appeared in the Fall of 1988 in Acadiana Profile Magazine. Reprinted with permission of Acadiana Profile.)

He was a congressman of integrity and intelligence who represented the interests of the people of the Third District of his state for eight years.

He was one of the leading citizens Louisiana has produced this century.

Born in Lafayette, La., on Jan. 6, 1907, Domengeaux was one of many descendants of the legendary Acadian, Jean Mouton, founder of the city of Lafayette.

Jimmie, as he was known to friends and acquaintances on both sides of the Atlantic, was the third son of Joseph R. and Marthe Domengeaux (nee Mouton). Jimmie was a descendant of Jean Mouton on his mother's side.

Before achieving a measure of prosperity as a planter in the 1820s, Jean Mouton had known great hardship. Like other Acadian pioneers, he had been deported by the British at the outset of the French and Indian War. His homeland, Acadia, now forms part of the Canadian province of Nova Scotia.

A second and more numerous wave of French refugees arrived in Louisiana at the turn of the 18th century. Coming from the Caribbean, they mingled with the Acadians, who had preceded them. On his father's side, Jimmie descended from Jean Francois Domengeaux, who had escaped from Haiti, then known as "the French part of Santo Domingo," during the rebellion led by Toussaint L'Ouverture.

With this blend of Cajun and Creole forebears, Jimmie was well-qualified to represent the French-speaking element of Louisiana. Under his leadership, the movement for the preservation and enhancement of the French heritage of Louisiana served notably to unite rather than divide the people of the state. Organizing and directing this ambitious undertaking engaged Jimmie's energies and ingenuity for two decades and may be considered his third and crowning career. He served as chairman of CODOFIL from its founding in 1968 until his death in 1988.

Before becoming chairman of CODOFIL, Jimmie had already made a name for himself as a lawyer and politician. These two careers were the foundation of the third.

The law was his first and fundamental vocation. As a practicing lawyer, both criminal and civil, Jimmie assisted clients in all walks of life. In the days before legal aid had become institutionalized, lawyers were expected to contribute voluntarily of their time and talents to *pro bono* work. Jimmie did not shirk the obligation; on the contrary, he took satisfaction in it.

"There is still a standing rule in his law office," Louisiana Congressman Edward Hebert reported in March of 1974, "that anybody in the grip of loan sharks or finance companies shall be defended free of charge."

ABOUT THE AUTHOR: Philip F. Dur, 73, is a professor emeritus of political science at the University of Southwestern Louisiana in Lafayette, having taught the subject there from 1965 to 1984. He served in the U.S. Foreign Service from 1946 to 1965 in various capacities in France, Germany, Japan and Panama. He was in the U.S. Navy from 1942 to 1946. He's listed in Who's Who in America and American Men and Women of Science. He was awarded *Palmes Académiques* by the French government in 1973 and the Medal of Honor by the National Society of the Daughters of the American Revolution in 1983. A graduate of Harvard University, his articles have been published in numerous periodicals. Among his writings is a biography of the late Ambassador Jefferson Caffery. Some of the insights gained for this article on the life of James Domengeaux were gained in the author's tenure as an advisor to the Council for the Development of French in Louisiana, from 1968 to the present.

Educated in private schools and at the state college in Lafayette, then called Southwestern Louisiana Institute, Jimmie studied law at Loyola and Tulane universities in New Orleans. He was admitted to the bar and began the practice of law in Lafayette in 1932. The legal profession was rewarding for him in a material sense. His considerable personal fortune derived from legal fees, as well as shrewd investments.

He was in the great American tradition a self-made man. One of Jimmie's anecdotes, related by a French journalist, illustrates what is meant by the term. The Domengeaux family, like many others in south Louisiana, had been hard-hit by the Great Depression. Consequently Jimmie had to pay his own way as a student in New Orleans. Having left Lafayette with $5 in his pocket, he offered his services as a fireman on arrival in the big city. They were apparently accepted. Jimmie thus read law in the interval between fire alarms in the Crescent City.

Jimmie's private wealth was helpful to the French movement. Established by Act 409 of the State Legislature in 1968, CODOFIL was not funded for administrative purposes until two years later. As the unpaid chairman of the organization, Jimmie continued to draw on his own resources to supplement the rather meager allocations of public money for the costs of travel and representation involved in international relations. Over the years, a stream of distinguished visitors was attracted to Louisiana by CODOFIL, and CODOFIL, in turn, participated in a series of conferences and conventions abroad. One knowledgeable source estimates the sum of Jimmie's personal contributions to the expenses of CODOFIL at no less than $1 million. Since this figure corresponds to an expenditure of $50,000 per year for 20 years, it seems

"He was, in the great American tradition, a self-made man."

reasonable.

The bulk of CODOFIL's budget, averaging $2 million a year in the mid-1980s, was earmarked for language instruction in the elementary schools. Less than 20 percent was ordinarily available for the multiple costs of administration, such as the maintenance and staffing of the CODOFIL office in Lafayette, the provision of scholarships and travel grants to teachers and students, subsidies for broadcasting programs in French on television and for publishing a periodical in French. To defray these expenses a separate, private but non-profit organization was set up under the name of *Fondation CODOFIL* to solicit donations from the public. Thus it was hoped the French movement in Louisiana would not in the future be so heavily dependent on one man's philanthropy.

The adequacy or inadequacy of the CODOFIL budget is, of course, subject to review at every session of the Louisiana Legislature. Since an ambitious project of cultural development such as CODOFIL is something of a rarity in American politics at the state level, its funding naturally invites questions. What seems to be unquestionable is that CODOFIL would never have been funded by the State had it not been for Jimmie's undoubted political clout and integrity.

When Domengeaux said, "I'm clean," the words carried conviction. His entire political career was evidence of the truth of the statement, from the very beginning.

An outspoken critic of Huey Long when the Kingfish was at the zenith of his power, Jimmie remained a steadfast opponent of the Long machine after Huey's death in September of 1935. Jimmie was a young radio announcer who called attention to himself by broadcasting attacks on the Kingfish and his henchmen for their arbitrariness and corruption.

Having served one term in the State Legislature, Jimmie ran for the U.S. House of Representatives in 1940 following the outbreak of the "Louisiana Scandals," in which Huey's lieutenants were involved. The seamy side of Louisiana politics had then been starkly revealed by the mail fraud conviction of the governor, Richard W. Leche, a follower of Huey's.

Jimmie managed the campaign of the reform candidate for governor, Sam Houston Jones, in southwest Louisiana, while himself campaigning for the job of Congressman from the Third District. Sam Jones was elected governor with a narrow plurality over Huey's brother, Earl, in a run-off. Jimmie received a record majority of the vote in the first primary.

More popular in his own district than the man on whose ticket he was running, Jimmie was in large part responsible for Jones' good showing in south Louisiana. Even though derided by Earl Long as "High Hat Sam . . . not one of our rural kind," the "good government" candidate proved highly acceptable to Cajun farmers.

Domengeaux's enduring effectiveness as a community leader was attributable to the force of his own personality rather than to the favor of the bosses, whoever they might have been. Jimmie was a born political maverick. In this he took after his father. Joseph Rodolph Domengeaux, a veteran of the Spanish-American War and an admirer of Teddy Roosevelt, had been elected to the Louisiana Senate on the Bull Moose ticket, as the first, albeit dissident, Republican since Reconstruction, after Roosevelt had broken with Taft. The elder Domengeaux was subsequently re-elected to the same senate as a Democrat.

Jimmie's ties to the Democratic Party were no more constraining than had been his father's to the Republican. While remaining a Democrat, Jimmie was not exactly a follower of Franklin Delano Roosevelt. He resented Roosevelt's courtship of the Long machine in Louisiana, once Huey, a potential rival for the Presidency of the United States, had been eliminated by assassination.

An anecdote Jimmie once told explains the relationship between President and congressman. Following the Japanese attack on Pearl Harbor, which came in the midst of his first term in Congress, Jimmie, then 35 years old but a bachelor, was eager to enlist in the armed forces. From a partisan point of view, the impulse was to be resisted, for it would have reduced an already slim Democratic majority of two in the House. Alerted to Jimmie's intentions, the President summoned him to the White House. As Jimmie recalled their interview, Roosevelt, who prided himself on his knowledge of French, opened the conversation with a greeting in that language, assuming it no doubt to be his guest's mother tongue. If intended to conciliate the congressman from Louisiana, the gesture was ill-conceived. Domengeaux's tart reply was: "Mr. President, I can speak English, you know."

Roosevelt overlooked the rebuke, and Jimmie put off joining the army for a while, but relations between President and representative were never friendly.

Jimmie remembered Roosevelt's successor, Harry S. Truman, with affection and respect. As senator, Truman had been his card-playing partner.

They met regularly with other friends around the poker table on Friday nights. In contrast to FDR, Truman impressed Domengeaux as being a truly likeable man, spontaneous and unaffected, devoted to his friends.

For Sam Rayburn, veteran Speaker of the House, Jimmie also had little use. In his opinion "Mr. Sam" had conspired with Roosevelt to manipulate the Southern bloc in Congress, "directing Southern federal influence into Socialistic trends." Never one to mince words, Jimmie denounced some of the New Deal legislation retrospectively as likely "eventually to bring about the destruction of this nation."

Jimmie was re-elected to Congress in 1942. He then became the third congressman to resign his seat in order to serve in the armed forces. Like others among his colleagues, he could have taken military leave for the purpose, but he preferred to make a clean break. Enlisting in the army as a private in April of 1944, he was sent to Camp Shelby in Mississippi and assigned to the combat engineers. The arrangement was meant to be only temporary. He had been offered a commission by the Civil Affairs Division of the War Department upon completion of basic training.

However, his military career proved to be short-lived. Within less than two months of his enlistment he was given a medical discharge because of ulcers. The gastric disorder had been aggravated by army food and army bullying. Domengeaux had a drill sergeant who disliked Italians and took him for one.

"Get in line DiMaggio!" the invidious non-com would shout. "You're not in Congress anymore."

Joe DiMaggio, outfielder for the Yankees, was then at the height of his fame. The names DiMaggio and Domengeaux sounded alike, as usually pronounced. The confusion between

> *"Jimmie remembered President Harry S. Truman with affection and respect. As senator, Truman had been his card-playing partner. They met regularly with other friends around the poker table on Friday nights."*

them was sometimes more amusing than on the parade gound at Camp Shelby. Jimmie's younger brother recalls having been invited by Jimmie to watch the Joe Louis-Billy Conn fight in New York in 1941. The crowd milling around in the lobby of the Hotel New Yorker on that occasion heard somehow that DiMaggio was among them. On being asked if he was the famous baseball player, Jimmie replied with all modesty, "No, I'm only his younger brother."

In November of 1944 Jimmie resumed his political career by obtaining re-election to the seat he had vacated seven months previously. Thus succeeding himself, Jimmie ran for Congress a third time. Again he was returned from the Third District of Louisiana. Jimmie Davis, Sam Jones' handpicked successor, was then governor.

The following year Domengeaux married Eleanor St. Julien of Lafayette, whose father had served for many years as clerk of court and whose uncle had been mayor of Lafayette. The St. Juliens, like the Domengeauxs, were of pre-Revolutionary French origin. The marriage spanned all three of Jimmie's careers.

Jimmie was re-elected to Congress a fourth time in 1946. But when the elections of 1948 came around, the balance of political forces in Louisiana had

175

shifted dramatically. Earl Long had been elected governor in a run-off against Sam Jones in February. Earl's victory was overwhelming. A strong rival for Jimmie's seat in Congress consequently emerged in the person of Edwin Willis, a lawyer from St. Martinville devoted to the Longs. The principal political bosses in south Louisiana – Dudley LeBlanc, Leander Perez and others – were supporting Willis.

In preference to confronting the seemingly unbeatable Willis, Jimmie decided to run against the incumbent senator from Louisiana, Allen Ellender. Since Ellender, too, was a Longite, having served as Huey's Speaker of the Louisiana House of Representatives, he was no less formidable an opponent than Willis. In choosing to run against him, Domengeaux seemed to be seeking a more honorable way out. Losing a statewide race for the U.S. Senate might be considered somehow more honorable than being repudiated in one's home district.

Ironically, as it turned out, he might well have beaten Willis in spite of Earl Long's influence. The newly elected governor had succeeded in alienating the south Louisiana bosses between his election in February and the Congressional primary in August by his erratic and high-handed behavior. Jimmie's campaign for the Senate was, however, lackadaisical in the extreme, more of a gesture of defiance toward the Long machine than an all-out struggle for political survival. Instead of stumping the state, Jimmie spent the summer in New Orleans at the Hotel Monteleone with his young wife, awaiting the outcome of the balloting on August 31. His only foray for votes was to Donaldsonville, in the vicinity of New Orleans.

The returns of the first primary at the end of August were decisive. Ellender won with 61.7 percent of the vote. Domengeaux lost with 25.9 percent, carrying only one parish out of 64. Both Ellender and Willis were elected. The former went on to win election after election until he died in office. The latter served 20 years in Congress before being defeated in 1968. Having lost the election of 1948, Jimmie made no effort at a comeback. Henceforth he devoted himself to the practice of law in Lafayette and eventually to the leadership of the French movement.

When Jimmie again took up residence in Lafayette in 1948, it was a different city from the one he had left in 1941. Oil production in Louisiana had doubled between 1936 and 1946, and since 1947 offshore oil drilling had started in the Gulf. Lafayette was destined to become the headquarters of this new industry.

Jimmie's law firm was to pioneer in the extension of maritime law to the offshore rigs, thus indirectly encouraging the local population to seek employment in the oil industry. Offshore jobs were still hazardous, but the compensation for accidents increased and working conditions improved.

Industrial expansion interacting with universal conscription during two world wars had inevitably drawn the rural Cajuns into the American melting pot. Although more resistant to assimilation than the urban Creoles, the inhabitants of southwest Louisiana had grown out of the isolation which made them a people apart. Like other ethnic minorities in democratic countries during the 1960s, they were becoming more concerned with preserving their identity the nearer they came to losing it. In 1965 the bicentennial of the arrival of the Acadians was celebrated in Lafayette. The Cardinal Archbishop of Quebec was present for the occasion and said Mass in French at the cathedral.

Jimmie assumed the leadership of what is commonly called the "French movement" to bring the United States into closer relations with the French-speaking nations of the world. The goals of CODOFIL were defined as exclusively cultural and non-political.

"Preserve the language and you preserve the culture" was Jimmie's watchword from the beginning. The main thrust of the movement has accordingly been directed to promoting the teaching of French in the schools.

Jimmie was still a schoolboy in the 1920s when the school boards of the south Louisiana parishes decreed that French should not be spoken on the school grounds. Like others of his generation, Jimmie recalled how pupils were punished by their teachers for breaking this rule. One of the more cruel and unusual punishments consisted in being made to kneel for an hour at a time on scattered grains of corn.

Free, public and compulsory education had been instituted by law in Louisiana in 1916. But just as the opportunity to confer bilingual literacy on the children of the state appeared, it was rejected as a matter of policy. Domengeaux denounced this act of cultural obscurantism in no uncertain terms.

"The schools took French away from us," he is quoted as saying, "and we are largely responsible for this, because it was our own Acadian teachers who punished us for speaking French and refused to teach us about our language and culture – something that was within our right as free people living in a democratic society." Such was the situation CODOFIL set out to reverse.

Legislative Act 409 of July 20, 1968 establishing CODOFIL was preceded by Act 408 of the same date instituting French language instruction in the public schools of the state.

"As expeditiously as possible but not later than the beginning of the 1972-73 school year" all public elementary schools were to offer five years of French, beginning in the first grade. High schools were similarly required to teach French for three years. The latter requirement was not, however, put into effect. The law was by its own terms permissive instead of mandatory. School boards and individual parents have the right to opt out of the program at any time.

To Jimmie's intense disappointment, several of the most Acadian parishes of the state, such as Iberia, Lafourche, St. Mary, Terrebonne and Vermilion, did just that. To Jimmie's surprise and satisfaction, however, CODOFIL's program of language instruction proved to be as acceptable to north as to south Louisiana. More than half of the 66 school systems in the state are teaching French in the elementary grades, and the number of teachers of French is evenly distributed between north and south.

Such widespread acceptance of the educational reform pursued by CODOFIL would not have been possible if the enterprise had been controversial. Controversy would inevitably have been generated by any systematic attempt to impose French on the schools. Act 714 adopted by the legislature in July of 1975 is a case in point. This law closed the loophole in Act 408 by requiring school boards to offer second language instruction on the petition of 25 percent of the parents concerned. It has been invoked only once, by a young activist of the French movement who is also a lawyer. As a consequence, the school board of Jefferson Davis Parish was obliged to comply with the requirements of Act 408 and is now offering French in five grades of elementary education.

The number of public school students enrolled in French courses in Louisiana has fluctuated between 40,000 and 50,000 since the 1974-1975 school year. A peak of 51,800 was reached in 1982-1983. The causes of this lack of momentum are not political. All the enabling acts for CODOFIL programs were carried unanimously, thanks to the parliamentary skills of the state senator from Lafayette, Edgar Mouton, and to Jimmie's political influence. Mouton, who served as floor leader in the Louisiana Senate for Governor John McKeithen and later for Governor Edwin Edwards, was a family friend of the Domengeauxs.

The restrictions on CODOFIL's activity have come from the educational establishment, notably the school administrators, and the complications of the budgetary process. Act 714 was adopted without difficulty by the legislature, although it was opposed vehemently by the School Board Association and the Superintendent of Education. Bureaucrats and not politicians made problems for Jimmie.

In the American system of checks and balances between the executive and legislative powers, expenditures are more easily authorized than funded. Not until 1970 did the Louisiana Legislature appropriate any money for the administration of CODOFIL. For the first two years of its existence, therefore, the organization worked out of Jimmie's law office. Its only staff was a bilingual secretary, France Lemay, whom Jimmie had brought from Quebec. Thanks to Jimmie's and France's devoted efforts, CODOFIL survived its austere beginnings. But even in the years of swelling oil royalties and severance taxes, CODOFIL's budget continued to oscillate around $2 million, of which $300,000 is at present designated for administrative expenses.

Had it not been for foreign aid, the CODOFIL program of language instruction would never have gotten off the ground. Only $25,000 of State funds were available for education when CODOFIL began operations, and there were no qualified native teachers of French in the elementary schools.

At the organizational meeting of CODOFIL in October of 1968, over which Jimmie presided, the head of the foreign languages department of the University of Southwestern Louisiana (USL) in Lafayette was happy to announce that the first training course for native teachers of French at the elementary level had been given the previous summer. Lacking teachers and restricted in funds, the project to develop bilingualism in Louisiana threatened to be stillborn. The only recourse was to seek help abroad.

The legislature had indicated as much. Senate and House resolutions, adopted in 1967 and 1968 respectively, recommended closer relations between Louisiana and Canada, more specifically with the provinces of Quebec and New Brunswick, which contain the largest French-speaking populations. Act 409, moreover, provided that CODOFIL "may receive donations and grants from individuals, corporations and governments in order to further the provisions of this Act."

Acting on these hints, Jimmie went straight to the heads of government in Quebec and France. The resulting situation was mildly deprecated by Congressman Edward Hebert of Louisiana in 1974 at the same time as he extolled the success of CODOFIL's educational enterprise. It is admittedly anomalous for an American state to depend on foreign nations to educate its children, as Hebert observed, but no other option was available at the time.

Jimmie's venture in cultural diplomacy had the enthusiastic support of Gov. John McKeithen, under whose administration CODOFIL began. In September of 1969 they traveled together to Quebec to seek assistance for the French movement in Louisiana. McKeithen and Premier Jean-Jacques Bourrassa pledged themselves by joint press statement on this occasion to cultural and linguistic cooperation in the broadest terms. The practical consequences of their understanding had, however, still to be spelled out.

Accordingly, an Acadian from Canada by the name of Leo LeBlanc was sent to Lafayette to work with Domengeaux and inaugurate the official representation of the Quebec government in Louisiana. On a preliminary visit to Lafayette in July, however, LeBlanc had stated that Quebec's aid would be technical rather than financial.

In order to find and fund teachers of French for the schools of Louisiana, Jimmie turned to France. Two months after his return from Quebec, he flew to Paris. Bearing an invitation from the governor to the French President to visit Louisiana, Jimmie proposed to meet Georges Pompidou face to face. According to all accounts, the meeting was highly informal and entirely successful.

At the beginning of the next school year, 1970-1971, 30 teachers of French arrived in Louisiana from France. They were young men of military age who had chosen to serve in the French equivalent of the Peace Corps rather than undergo army training. The French designation for them was *coopérant*. Several of them brought their wives. Seventy more *coopérants* were added to the contingent the next year. By agreement with CODOFIL, the French gov-

> ## "CODOFIL has successfully implanted the French language in the schools from which it had been banished 60 years earlier."

ernment paid their travel expenses to and from Louisiana as well as half their monthly salaries. Thus it was possible to start teaching French in the elementary schools of Louisiana with the paltry allotment provided by the State.

Quebec in 1972 and Belgium in 1974 also arranged to supply teachers to Louisiana, and the number of foreign "associate" teachers of French in the elementary public schools of the state peaked at 232 in the school year 1974-1975. The French government stopped sending *coopérants* to Louisiana in 1975. Foreign teachers now receive the standard minimum salary of $12,700 per year from the State with whatever supplement of pay the parish school board may provide.

The economic incentive for the State to employ foreign teachers of French has thus vanished, while the number of native teachers qualified for second language teaching at the elementary level has increased, thanks to the certification programs developed by the state universities since 1973, following USL's lead. In the 1987-1988 school year, there were 169 of these second language specialists with diplomas from state universities teaching in grades one through eight and 96 associate teachers from abroad.

CODOFIL has thus successfully implanted the French language in the schools from which it had been banished 60 years earlier. The resistance of administrators to the inclusion of a second language in the elementary curriculum has gradually dwindled. In

1984 the Board of Elementary and Secondary Education (BESE) itself mandated a five-year program of foreign language instruction for grades four through eight. Implementation was to begin in the fourth grade and extend by one grade a year until the requirement was fulfilled. French is not the only foreign language offered. Spanish, Italian and Hungarian have been added to the curriculum, but 90 percent of the students in foreign languages take French.

As might be expected, execution of BESE's order has been hindered by budgetary restrictions, but funding is supposed to come from the royalties of offshore oil production heretofore held in escrow by the federal government and recently awarded to the State. Louisiana is committed to using the money for the support of public education.

The propagation of French by the mass media which Jimmie described as indispensable in 1970 has likewise not been neglected. Legislative Act 458 of July of 1968 purported to set up in collaboration with USL, a non-profit television station to broadcast in French. This law has remained a dead letter, but, with subsidies from CODOFIL, Louisiana Public Broadcasting has since 1981 scheduled four hours of programming in French per week. Acadiana Open Channel also broadcasts French television programs once a week. Commercial radio stations broadcast in French about 100 hours a week, while station KRVS on the USL campus is a bilingual radio station airing programs in French for about 40 hours a week.

The dream of teaching an entire generation to speak French, however, has faded. As President Pompidou is reported to have said to Jimmie in 1969, "It has taken 100 years to suppress French in Louisiana; you won't be able

> **"The growing interest in Cajun culture is a by-product of the struggle to save Louisiana's French language and heritage."**

to restore it in ten."

From the beginning, CODOFIL's concentration on bilingual education reflected more than concern for the preservation of a cultural heritage. The French movement was also animated by the hope that the cultivation of Louisiana's native French tongue could open a new channel of communication between the United States and the outside world. The vision persists as a distant goal but not an unattainable one. In fact, the passage of time has only pointed up the desirability of the project.

An "intimate" knowledge of his language is the key to understanding a foreigner's point of view, Jimmie once observed. As leader of the French movement, Jimmie also demonstrated in his personal experience that by speaking the language of a country one can win the confidence of its people.

In Louisiana itself, CODOFIL's effort to preserve the mother tongue of one-third of the population has engendered a cultural revolution. Insofar as it has not been fatally anglicized, Louisiana French is, as Domengeaux and others have described it, a variant of the language spoken by the early settlers of the state. It is readily understood by other French-speaking peoples of the Caribbean, of Canada, of Europe and Africa.

Cajun culture, however, is something unique, blending French, Spanish, African and Amerindian elements in various proportions. In its culinary and musical aspects particularly, this culture is now appreciated both at home and abroad. Cajun chefs have opened restaurants in New York, and Cajun bands have played in Paris. In the academic environment, notably at USL, Cajun studies are flourishing. The inhabitants of south Louisiana are discovering their roots. The publicity generated by Domengeaux's cultural diplomacy, moreover, has drawn numerous tourists from Canada and France. The interest displayed by these visitors from abroad, as well as that shown by fellow Americans, has stimulated the Cajuns' pride in themselves and their heritage. The growing interest in Cajun culture is thus a by-product of the struggle to save Louisiana's French language and heritage. It is perhaps the most certain achievement of the French movement under Jimmie Domengeaux's leadership.

This prophet was recognized in his own land

The quality of Jimmie Domengeaux's leadership has been recognized both at home and abroad. The ancient saying that a prophet is not without honor save in his own land does not hold in his case.

The long series of honors conferred upon him for his contributions to the cultural development of Louisiana and to the furtherance of international understanding began in 1973. In that year he was awarded the degree of doctor of humanities by the College of Notre Dame in Manchester, N.H., and made an officer of the Legion of Honor by the French government.

Many other distinctions came to him later, including these: the honorary doctorate of civil law, bestowed upon him by the University of Moncton, New Brunswick, in 1975; his decoration as an officer of the Order of Leopold by the King of the Belgians in 1978; the certificate of merit he received from the Louisiana Department of Education in 1980; the doctorates of humane letters granted him by Loyola University of New Orleans in 1984 and by Louisiana State University in 1986. In the same year, he was promoted to the rank of commander in the Legion of Honor, aptly termed "one of the most prestigious honors that France can bestow." The honor was doubled in 1987 when Jimmie became commander in the Belgian Order of the Crown.

In addition to these tributes from governments and universities, Jimmie has won the admiration and gratitude of his fellow citizens. New testimony to this effect was provided in 1988 when the *Festival International de Louisiane* was dedicated to Jimmie Domengeaux. This annual cultural event, jointly planned and organized by public and private agencies of the city and parish of Lafayette and of the state of Louisiana, is intended to exhibit the vibrant Cajun style in all its aspects — artistic, literary, musical and culinary — with the participation of performing artists from Africa, Belgium, Canada, France and Haiti.

As a manifestation of the vitality of Louisiana's French heritage and its international resonance, the festival was a recognition of Jimmie's wholehearted dedication to the French movement in Louisiana.

Bibliography

Arsenault, Bona. *History of the Acadians* (Quebec, 1966).

Beers, Henry P. *The French in North America* (Baton Rouge, La., 1957).

Bird, Harrison. *Navies in the Mountains* (New York, 1962).

Bolton, Herbert Eugene. *Athanase de Mezieres and the Louisiana-Texas Frontier, 1768-1780* (2 Vols., Cleveland, 1914).

Boudreau, Amy. *The Story of the Acadians* (New Orleans, 1955).

Brebner, J. B. *Canada: A Modern History* (Ann Arbor, Mich., 1960).

Brebner, J. B. *The Explorers of North America* (Garden City, N.Y., 1933).

Burpee, Lawrence J. *The Search for the Western Sea* (Toronto, Canada, 1935).

Clark, Andrew H. *Acadia: The Geography of Early Nova Scotia to 1760* (Madison, Wisc., 1968).

Colden, Cadwallader. *History of the Five Indian Nations of Canada which Are Dependent on the New York Province...* (Ithaca, N.Y., reprint, 1973).

Costain, Thomas B. *The White and the Gold: The French Regime in Canada* (Garden City, N.Y., 1954).

Crouse, Nellis M. *La Verendrye, Fur Trader and Explorer* (Ithaca, N.Y., 1956).

Davis, Edwin A. *Louisiana: A Narrative History* (Baton Rouge, La., 1961).

Deiler, J. H. *The Settlement of the German Coast of Louisiana and the Creoles of German Descent* (Baltimore, Md., 1969).

Dufour, Charles L. *Ten Flags in the Wind: The Story of Louisiana* (New York, 1967).

Dunn, Jacob F. "The Mission to the Ouabach," in *Indiana Historical Society Publications*, Vol. III, No. 4, Page 94.

Eastman, Mack. *Church and State in Early Canada* (Edinburgh, 1915).

Eccles, William J. *The Canadian Frontier, 1534-1760* (New York,1969).

Eccles, William J. *France in America* (New York, 1972).

Edmonds, Walter D. *The Musket and the Cross* (New York, 1968).

Foley, William E. *A History of Missouri, Vol. 1, 1673 to 1820* (Columbia, Mo., 1971).

Foreman, Grant. "Antoine Leroux, New Mexico Guide," in *New Mexico Historical Review*, Vol. XVI, Pages 367-77 (Santa Fe, N.M., October, 1941).

Hamilton, Raphael N. *Marquette's Explorations: The Narratives Re-examined* (Madison, Wisc., 1970).

Havighurst, Walter. *Three Flags at the Straits* (Englewood Cliffs, N.J., 1962).

Hunt, George T. *The Wars of the Iroquois* (Madison, Wisc., 1940).

Innes, Harold A. *The Fur Trade in Canada* (New Haven, Conn., 1930).

Kellogg, Louise P. *The French Regime in Wisconsin and the Northwest* (Madison, 1935).

Kinietz, Vernon. *The Indians of the Western Great Lakes* (Ann Arbor, Mich., 1965).

Lanctot, Gustave A. *A History of Canada, Vols. 1 and 2* (New York, 1960-1964).

LeBlanc, Dudley J. *The Acadian Miracle* (Lafayette, La., 1966).

Le Sueur, William D. *Count Frontenac* (Toronto, Ontario, 1964).

Marshall, Thomas R. "St. Vrain's Expedition to the Gila in 1826," in *Southwestern Historical Quarterly*, Vol. XIX, No. 3, Pages 251-60 (Austin, Tex., January, 1916).

Martin, Francois-Xavier. *The History of Louisiana* (New Orleans, La., 1963).

McDermott, John F., ed. *Frenchmen and French Ways in the Mississippi Valley* (Urbana, Ill., 1969).

McGinty, Garnie W. *A History of Louisiana* (New York, 1951).

Miller, Perry. *The New England Mind from Colony to Province* (Boston, 1953).

Morison, Samuel E. *The European Discovery of America: The Northern Voyages, A.D. 500-600* (New York, 1971).

Morison, Samuel E. *Samuel de Champlain, Father of New France* (New York, 1972).

Morton, Arthur S. *A History of the Canadian West* (Toronto, Ontario, 1939).

Nasatir, Abraham P. *Before Lewis and Clark* (2 Vols., St. Louis, 1952).

Nasatir, Abraham P. and Loomis, Noel M. *Pedro Vial and the Roads to Santa Fe* (Norman, Okla., 1967)

Parkman, Francis. *The Conspiracy of Pontiac and the Indian War after the Conquest of Canada* (Collier Edition, New York, 1962).

Parkman, Francis. *LaSalle and the Discovery of the Great West* (Signet Edition, New York, 1963).

Quimby, George I. *Indian Culture and European Trade Goods* (Madison, Wisc., 1966).

Robinson, Percy J. *Toronto During the French Regime* (Toronto, Ontario, 1965).

Rutledge, Joseph L. *A Century of Conflict* (New York, 1956).

Sandoz, Mari. *The Beaver Men* (New York, 1964).

Steck, Francis B. *The Joliet-Marquette Expedition* (Quincy, Ill., 1928).

Thwaites, R. G., ed. *The Jesuit Relations and Allied Documents* (Reprint Edition, New York, 1959).

Van Osdal, A.L. *Historic Land Mark* (Yanktown, S.D., 1915).

Wheat, Carl L. *Mapping the Trans-Mississippi West* (Vol. I, San Francisco, 1957).

Winzerling, Oscar W. *The Acadian Odyssey* (Baton Rouge, La., 1955).

Zoltvany, Yves F., ed. *The French Tradition in America* (University of South Carolina Press, Columbia, 1969).

INDEX

—A—

Abenaki Indians, 90, 92, 93
Acadia, 28, 29, 32, 37,39
Acadian Odyssey, 147
Acadian Peninsula, 15, 18, 25, 129
Alexander, Sir William, 32, 36
Algonquin Indians, 59, 63, 65, 70
American Revolution, 140
Amite River, 108
Anacosti, 22
Andaste Indians, 76
Annapolis Basin, 29
Annapolis Valley, 31, 131
Appalachian Highlands, 159
Argall, Samuel, 31
Arkansas River, 160
Ascension Parish, 144
Assumption Parish, 144
Aubry, Charles, 137
Aunis, 139

—B—

Baird, Rev. Pierre, 30
Baltimore, 134
Bartlett, John Russell, 167
Baton Rouge, 107
Bayou Manchac, 107, 108
Bayougoula Indians, 105-107
Beaubassin, 132, 133
Beauvoir-sur-Mer, 40
Beaver, 26
Bernard, André, 40
Biencourt, Charles, 30-32
Bienville, Jean-Baptiste de, 105, 108, 110, 112, 114, 123, 124, 162-164
Blanchard, Anselmo, 143
Blanchard, Guillaume, 50
Boston, 133
Boudrot, Michel, 40
Boundary Creek, 50
Bourgeois, Jacques, 40, 48
Bourgmond, Etienne de, 162, 163
Brazos River, 102

Breda, Treaty of, 37, 41
Bristol, 13, 14
Brittany, 139, 141
Broussard, Alexandre, 50
Broussard, Joseph, 50, 137
Bruyere, Fabry de la, 164
Brule, Etienne, 56, 61, 158
Brule River, 78
Burel, Gilbert, 67

—C—

Caboto, Giovanni (John Cabot), 14
Cadillac, Governor, 115, 116, 161
Canada, 32, 40, 41
Canseau, 15, 25
Cape Breton Island, 14, 15, 38
Cape Fear River, 22
Cape François, St. Domingue, 105, 114
Cape Race, 22
Cape Sable, 38, 42
Carignan Regiment, French Army, 41, 49, 76
Cartier, Jacques, 22,23
Casey, Roger, 40
"Casket Girls," 123
Cathedral of St. Louis, 124
Cayuga Indians, 76
Census of 1671, 41-47
Census of 1724, 122
Champlain, Samuel de, 26-29, 31, 55-57, 65, 158
Charbonneau, Toussant, 165
Charles Fort, 32
Charles, King, 57
Charles III, King, 140,141
Charton, François, 67
Chauvin, Pierre, 23,
Cherbourg, 36
Choctaw Indians, 108, 124
Codfish, 14, 15, 18, 21
Colbert, Jean-Baptiste, 40-42, 49, 75, 85

Columbus, 14
Compagnie de St. Sacrament, 59
Company of New France, 59
Cook, Col. Philip St. George, 167
Cormier, Robert, 40
Cornwallis, Sir Edward, 130
Coudreniére, Peyroux de la, 140-142, 145
Count de Aranda, 140-143, 147
Count de Vergennes, Charles Gravier, 141
Coureurs de Bois, 32, 42, 61, 62, 86, 112, 158-161, 168
Crozat, Antoine, 115-118
Cruzatte, Peter, 165
Cumberland Basin, 48, 49

—D—

Dale, Thomas, 31
Daniel, Rev. Antoine, 71
D'Aspres, Manuel, 142, 146, 147
D'Aulnay, Madame, 36
D'Aulnay, Sieur, 33-35, 38
Davion, Rev. Antoine, 111
De Boisbriant, Pierre du Gue, 111
De Brebeuf, Rev. Jean, 67, 71
De Brion-Chabot, Philippe, Admiral of France, 22
De Charlevoix, Rev. Pierre, 157
De Chastes, Aymar, 26, 27
De Groseilliers, Medart Chouart, 75
De la Noue, Rebutel, 160
De la Perier Salvert, Etienne Boucher, 123, 124
De la Roche, Marquis, 23
De Medici, Catherine, 30
De Montigny, Rev. François, 111
De Monts, Sieur, 27-29, 55
De Noyon, Jacques, 160
De Pauger, Adrien, 118
De Salazar, Jacques, 30, 31
De Soulanges, Joybert, 41
D'Entremont, Philippe Mius, 36, 40, 42
Denys, Nicholas, 33, 34, 37, 42
Des Plaines River, 87, 90
Detroit River, 27, 88
D'Hauterive, Antoine Bernard, 137

D'Iberville, Pierre LeMoyne, 102, 104-108, 110, 113, 114, 157, 159
Di Tonti, Henri, 86, 87, 89, 90, 92, 94, 96, 97, 101, 106, 108, 111, 112, 157, 163
Dieppe, 14, 22, 29, 30, 102
D'Obleau, Rev. Jean, 67
Doiron, Pierre, 165
Donaldsonville, 144
Dotchet Island, 29
Doucette, Charles, 166
Du Plessis, Rev. Pacifique, 67
Du Sable, Jean Baptiste, 168
Du Tisne, Charles Claude, 162
Duc de Vandadour, 59
Duluth, 78
Duval, Jean, 56
Dykes, 51

—E—

England, 13, 37

—F—

Fécamp, 14
Ferdinand & Isabella of Spain, 13
Fleche, Rev. Jesse, 30
Forest, Michael, 40
Fort Crévecoeur, 87, 89, 90
Fort Frontenac, 85, 86, 89
Fort Maurepas, 108, 110-113, 157
Fort Orange, 70
Fort St. Louis de la Mobile, 113
Fox Indians, 90
Fox River, 59
France, 26, 37, 40
Francis I, King, 21, 22
Franciscans, 67, 167
François, Rev. Jean, 138
Fremont, Gen. John C., 167
French & Indian War, 133
Frontenac, Governor, 84, 92, 101, 163
Fundy, Bay of 28, 29, 36

—G—

Gálvez, Don Bernardo de, 141
Gálvez, José de, 141, 142
Gaspé, 22
Green Bay, 59, 86, 90

Georgian Bay, 68
Germans, 120, 122
"Grâce à Dieu", 30
Grandfontaine, Chevalier de, 41
Grand Pré, 49, 50, 131-133
Great Khan, 14
Guadeloupe, 136
Gulf of Mexico, 97, 108, 157
Gunnison, Capt. John W., 167
Guyenne, 139

—H—
Halifax, 130
Hamilton, Ontario, 84
Hare Island, 27
Harfleur, 14
Hebert, Louis, 31
Henry IV, King, 24, 26
Henry VII, King, 14
Hiawatha, 64
Hochelaga, 22
Honfleur, 14, 56
Houma Indians, 97, 107, 108
Hudson River, 58, 64, 65
Huguenot, 27, 30
Huron Indians, 59, 64, 65, 68, 70, 71,
    74, 75, 158

—I—
Iberia Parish, 137
Iberville, Pierre LeMoyne, 102, 104-
    108, 110, 113, 114, 157, 159
Illinois Indians, 87
Illinois River, 87
Ireland, 14
Iroquois, 58-60, 64, 70, 74-76, 85, 89,
    90, 92
Istrouma, 107
Italians, 13

—J—
Jamay, Rev. Denis, 67
James I, King, 32
Jemseg, 33, 35, 36, 41, 42
Jesuit, 30, 77, 102, 157, 158, 167
Jogues, Rev. Isaac, 69, 70
Joliet, Louis, 77, 78, 85, 94, 110
Jusseaume, René, 165

—K—
Kankakee River, 87, 90
Kickapoo Indians, 78, 90
Kingston, Ontario, 85
Kirke, Capt. David, 57

—L—
La Cadie, 28
"La Caroline," 147, 152
La Chausée, 39
"La Dauphine," 21
LaFrance , Joseph, 160
La Harpe, Bernard, 162
La Heve, 15, 25, 34, 39, 42
La Prée Ronde, 32
La Rochelle, 28, 31, 85, 146
"La Ville d'Archangel," 146, 152
Laclede, Pierre, 167
Lafayette Parish,137
Lafourche Parish, 124, 144
Lajeunesse, Basil, Charles &
    Francois,167
Lake Champlain, 65
Lake Erie, 27, 88
Lake George, 65
Lake Huron, 86, 102
Lake Maurepas, 108
Lake Michigan, 59, 86, 90
Lake Ontario, 27, 84, 85
Lake Pontchartrain, 108, 118
Lake Superior, 77, 160
Lalemant, Rev. Charles, 67
"La Amistad," 146, 151
"L'Amitié," 146, 151
Landry, Joseph, 166
Laramie River, 167
Laroque, François Antione, 165
LaSalle, Sieur de, René Robert
    Cavalier, 83, 85-90, 92-94, 96-98,
    101-103,106, 107, 159, 160, 167
Latour, Charles de, 32-38
Latour, Madame, 35
Law, John, 117, 118, 120, 123
Lawrence, Charles, 130, 131, 133
"Le Beaumont," 145, 149
"Le Bergère," 144, 148
"Le Bon Papa," 143, 148
LeBorgne, Emmanuel, 36, 37, 50

Le Caron, Rev. Joseph, 67
"Le Fleur de May," 30
"Le Griffon," 86-89
Le Havre, 14
LeSueur, Pierre, 161, 164
LeMoyne, Charles, 102
Leroux, Antoine, 167
Lewis & Clark, 160, 164
Long House Indians, 59, 64, 76
Louis XIV, King, 35, 86
Louisiana 93, 136, 157

—M—

Mackenzie, Alexander, 165
Mackinac Indians, 91
Madrid, 143
Malaria, 119
Mallet, Paul, 163, 164
Mallet, Pierre, 163, 164
Manhattan Island, 58
Marquess of Guercheville, Antoinette de Pons, 30
Marquette, Rev. Jacques, 77, 78, 85, 94, 110, 159, 160
Marseilles, 86
Marsolet, Nicholas, 56
Martin, Mathieu, 49
Martin, Pierre, 39
Martinique, 136
Maryland, 133, 134, 136
Massachusetts Colony, 32
Masse, Rev. Ennemond, 30, 67
Massignon, Genevieve, 39
Mediterranean, 13
Melancon, Pierre, 49
Memberton, 30
Memramcock River, 49
Menard, Pierre, 165
Mexico, 21
Miami Indians, 78, 92
Micmac Indians, 18-20, 28, 29, 135
Miró, Esteban, Gov., 143
Mission of the Martyrs, 70
Mississippi, 136
Mississippi River, 104, 136, 157, 159, 160
Missouri River, 157, 160
Mobile Bay, 105, 118, 121

Mobile River, 105, 113
Mohawk Indians, 64, 69, 70, 76
Mohegan Indians, 90, 92, 93
Montagnais Indians, 63, 65
Montreal, 22, 60, 75, 84, 158
Motin, Jeanne, 39
Motin, Louis, 39
Mougoulacha Indians, 105, 108
Mount Royal, 22

—N—

Nantes, 140
Naples, 86
Natchez Indians, 96, 97, 111, 123, 124
Natchitoches, 116, 161
Natel, Antoine, 56
Navarro, Martin, 143, 145, 147
New Brunswick, 33
New England, 90
New Mexico, 159, 161
New Orleans, 118, 121, 124
New York, 58
Newfoundland, 14, 15, 22
Niagara Falls, 27
Niagara River, 84, 88, 89
Nicolet, Jean, 59
Normandy, 139, 141
Normans, 14, 21
Northwest Passage to India, 21, 22, 57
Nova Scotia, 130, 135

—O—

Ohio River, 84, 92
Onendaga, 76
Opelousas, 137
Ottawa River, 57, 59
Ottawa Indians, 76, 91

—P—

Paris, 22
Pascagoula River, 110
Passamaquoddy, 42
Penicaut, André Joseph, 111, 120
Pennsylvania, 133
Penobscot, Maine, 31, 41
Pensacola Bay, 104, 105
Pentagoet, 38, 42
Peoria Lake, 87

Pesselin, Isaac, 39
Petitcoudiac River, 49, 50
Picardy, 28
Pineville, 124
Pisquid, 131-133
Pontchartrain, Jerome Phelypeaux, 104
Pontgrave, 23, 26-29, 55
Port Royal, 29-31, 35, 36, 38, 39, 41, 42, 133
Portuguese, 15
Potawatomi Indians, 90-92
Poutrincourt, 28, 29, 31
Poutrincourt, Madame de, 30
Press Gangs, 119
Protestant Merchants, 30
Provost, Etienne, 167
Puritans, 90

—Q—

Quebec, 22, 27, 41, 65, 75, 76, 84

—R—

Radisson, Pierre Esprit, 75
Ramee, Jacques de la, 167
Razilly, Isaac de. 32-34,
Recollets, 67
Red River, 97, 112, 160, 161
Richelieu, Cardinal, 32, 34
Roberval, Sieur de, 22, 23
Robidoux, Antoine, Francois, Joseph, Louis & Michel, 166
Rouen, 14, 26, 28
Russia, 26

—S—

Saint-Etienne, Claude de la Tour de, 30
Saint-Germain-en-Laye, Treaty of, 32
"Saint-Jehan," 39
Saint John River, 33, 38, 50
Saint-Sauveur, 30
Santa Fe Trail, 164
Santa Maria de Galve, 105
Seneca Indians, 64, 76
Shawnee Indians, 84, 92
Shoshone Indians, 160

Sieur d'Autray, 93, 97
Sieur de la Forest, François Daupin, 89, 90
Sieur de Maisonneuve, 59
Sieur de Tracy, 76
Sieur du L'Hut, Daniel Greysolon, 77, 160
Sieur Sauvole de la Villantray, 105, 108, 110-112, 125
Sioux Indians, 98, 159-161
Sitgreaves, Capt. Lorenzo, 167
Smallpox, 76
Spain, 13
Spainiards, 21
St. Croix River, 29, 78
St. Denis, Louis Juchereau de, 111, 112, 115, 161
St. Ignace, 71, 74, 86
St. Jean de Luz, 28
St. John's, Newfoundland, 23, 25
St. Joseph River, 86, 88-90
St. Lawrence River, 15, 22, 23, 25, 27, 31, 57, 59, 89, 159
St. Lawrence Valley, 75
St. Louis, 71
St. Louis River, 78
St. Malo, 22, 23, 28
St. Marie, 68, 74
St. Marie du Sault, 77
St. Martin Parish, 137
St. Martinville, 145
St. Mary Parish, 137
"St. Remi," 146, 150
Sulpician Order, 83

—T—

Tadousac, 15, 23, 25-27, 55, 56
Tensas Indians, 94, 97, 111
Tensas River, 105
Terriot, Pierre, 49
Terrebonne Parish, 144
Terrio, Oliver, 140, 144
Texas, 161
Thibodeau, Pierre, 50
Toulon, 86
Trahan, Guillaume, 39
Treaty of Paris, 133
Treaty of Ryswick, 103, 104

Treaty of 1763, 139
Treaty of Utrect, 129
Trois Rivieres, 48, 59, 70, 75, 158
Truteau, Pierre, 165
Tunica Indians, 111
Tunica Island, 108

—U—
Unzaga Y Amezaga, Luis, 140

—V—
Vallière, Michel LeNeuf de la, 48, 49
Venice, 14
Verendrye, Pierre Gaultier de la, 160
Vermilion Parish, 137
Verrazano, Giovanni da, 21, 22
Versailles, 86
Vial, Pierre, 164

Vieux Carre, 118
Ville Marie de Montreal, 59
Virginia, 31

—W—
War of Austrian Succession, 130
West Indies, 41
Wild-Rice Indians, 78
Winnebago Indians, 59
Winzerling, Oscar, 147
Winsconsin River, 78

—Y—
Yellow Fever, 119

—Z—
Zénobe, Father, 93, 98

Want to know more
about Louisiana's French heritage and culture?

Much of what you may want to know about Louisiana's French heritage and culture can be found in the pages of *Acadiana Profile*, "The Magazine of the Cajun Country," and in its special issues, cookbooks, tour guide and other fine products. For example:
- "The Origin of South Louisiana Family Names"
- "In Search of a Friendly Land"
- "The Character of the Cajun Country" (A pictorial)
- *Cajun Cooking* Cookbook (A set of two)
- *The Truth About the Cajuns* (A Book)
- Cajun Country Tour Guide & Festival Guide

For a free brochure, write to: *Acadiana Profile*, P.O. Box 52247, Lafayette, La. 70505.

Additional copies of *Louisiana's French Heritage* can also be ordered through Acadiana Profile.